In the beginning

was the Word

and so shall it be again,

and the Word

is the Law,

and the Law

is Love.

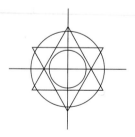

An Arimathean Foundation Healing Handbook

From the same publisher:

The Way of Love
Joseph of Arimathea Tells the True
Story behind the Message of Christ
Compiled by Peter Wheeler
ISBN 90-75635-01-X. 256pp
(Also available in Dutch)

The Way of Truth
ISBN 0-9532007-3-6
Compiled by Graham Timmins

The Memories of Josephes
Soul Memories of a Cousin of Jesus
David Davidson
ISBN 0-9532007-0-1. 256pp

The Children of Light
Father Abraham on the Fulfilment of a Prophecy
Compiled by David Davidson
ISBN 0-9532007-2-8. 96pp
(Monograph, also available in Dutch)

The Way of Soul
Compiled by David Davidson
ISBN 0-9532007-4-4. 128pp
(Monograph)

Discourses with Malachi
Opening to spiritual guidance
David Davidson
ISBN 0-9532007-6-0. 128pp
(Monograph)

In preparation:
The Way of Diet and Health
Compiled by Rosalind Pencherek
(Arimathean Healing Handbook)

For an order form send a stamped, self-addressed envelope to:
The Leaders Partnership, Box 16457,
London, SW14 5WH.

THE WAY
OF CRYSTALS

Compiled by Zanne Findlay

This book is dedicated to my two sons,
Andrew and Robert.

You may feel that this is magic, but why should there not be magic within the world? Is it really so impossible to imagine, that one of the most ancient minerals to be found within the surface of the Earth still has this magic, and has the power to be able to help and cure man?

The Arimathean

Many people have helped in the compilation of
this book, by searching through transcripts and
typing up trances and generally sharing their
expertise. In particular I would like to thank:

Anatole Beams for his creativity and goodwill
Su Kolevski for her willing and heartfelt support
Nina Parmar for her timely and excellent assistance
Rosalind Pencherek a sister in crystals and in life
Daniella Pencherek for her work behind the scenes
Elizabeth Price for making the spoken word so accessible
Josef Schmied for his attention to detail
Judith Timmins for her brilliance in shaping the text
Peter Wheeler, series editor and rock
ED for her extraordinary talent and last,
but certainly not least, David Davidson
soul mate and partner.

Front cover: The colours are from dyed agates, viewed
through a Chesnik Koch kaleidoscope and integrated
into a graphic image of a crystal.

Book design by Anatole Beams, Digital Media

Published by The Leaders Partnership,
PO Box 16457, London, SE14 5WH, UK
a non-profit publishing venture.
Web site: www.arimathea.com
ISBN 0-9532007-5-2

LP and the star design are trade
marks of the Leaders Partnership

First edition 2000. Printed in the UK
by Redwood Books, Trowbridge, Wiltshire.
Set in 11 on 12.6 point Galliard

The Way of Crystals

Index of exercises and practice guidelines

Foreword

I am waiting for a crystal healing, lying on a massage table in the basement of the author's home, which has been turned into a healing sanctuary. The walls are lined with shelves that are filled with beautiful crystals of every shape, size, colour and texture. But it is not these that she uses for her healing work – her healing stones are few; not polished or large or even particularly beautiful, they have been chosen for their energy rather than their looks. They are lying, carefully prepared, on a small table next to the wall.

My eyes are closed and I can hear her moving around the room. She places two long planks on special supports at either side of the bed and then, with one hand over my body, starts to place the crystals on them at strategic points. I can feel the energy change as she does so. Slowly I feel my body relax, I feel safe, my breathing becomes easy and deep and my heart rate slows down.

I hear her place the last crystal and she comes round and sits quietly at my head. She says nothing, the crystals say all that needs to be said. I gradually become aware of a profound stillness. I lose consciousness of the passing of time. Images start to flicker through my mind, I see healing colours moving gently behind my eyes, it is as if the crystals permit access to another realm, a spiritual realm where everything is now, a realm of gentleness and peace.

I feel as if I am part of the stones themselves, as still and enduring as a stone. Nothing matters in the way that it did before, my problems and pains gain a new meaning, a new perspective, and slip away. After what seems like forever I hear Zanne gently calling my name and gradually I re-surface. I listen with my eyes closed as she removes the crystals, hear her placing them into the sink under running water to cool and cleanse them. Surprisingly, I feel gratitude towards them, they have earned their bath.

This healing session was conducted exactly as the words in this book describe it. It is just one of the many techniques that are contained within this unique volume. Unique because this book combines the words of two spiritual masters, both with a profound insight into crystals and crystal healing, who have never before been published on this subject. Their words, woven together with the practical experience of Zanne Findlay, herself a crystal healer and teacher, make this book extremely authoritative at the same time as being simple, clear and pragmatic.

Each one of the techniques presented here has been proven by the author who has tried and tested them both on her courses and with individual clients. Because of this she has been able to balance the spiritual teachings of the Masters with her own insights into the problems and practicalities of applying the principles and techniques. As one who has directly benefited from the healing methods described here, I can wholeheartedly recommend this book.

David Davidson, Summer 2000

Introduction

*With the coming of the Golden age the crystals will, once again, become
important within the healing disciplines and therefore this journey
of rediscovery which you are beginning is just that – a journey.*

The Arimathean

This handbook is based on the teachings provided through a deep-trance
medium* who for the last twenty-five years has been providing channelled spiritual teachings of a very high quality. She wishes to remain anonymous.

At first one Teacher, known simply as 'The Master', spoke through her
and provided a wealth of material, some of which is contained within this handbook. In 1988 he made it clear that he was, in a previous life, Joseph of Arimathea, the uncle and guardian of Yeshua, who was to become Jesus the
Christ. As a spiritual master he now acts as a spokesperson for a group of souls
on the causal plane. In addition to the Master, this medium now also channels
the Prophet Elijah and Father Abraham. Part of their reason for working with
a channel is to provide a body of knowledge on the nature of Universal Law
and spiritual truth to help humanity to prepare for the profound changes that
will be affecting the planet in the next few decades.

The source

When this book was written in 2000, 'The Master' (who I refer to as 'The Arimathean') had been speaking for over twenty-five years. Many of the talks have
been transcribed into teaching transcripts some of which have formed the basis
of the books mentioned on page 159. A number of these talks are on the
nature of crystals and their healing potential. Some years later the Prophet
Elijah offered a number of trances specifically on crystals because he has a very
particular role in relation to them. As The Arimathean explains:

*Elijah has for at least one hundred years been energising crystals as they have been
mined and a market found for them. At that time he did not have voice but he
had presence and he had beauty. This was placed into crystals worldwide. First he
energised that which surrounded the Earth and within its composition, so that the
Earth would resonate with the beauty that it is capable of emitting.*

---

*A deep-trance channel is one who is literally 'entranced' by the Teachers who speak through
them. It is a very particular talent that takes many years to develop; to be able to surrender voluntarily to unconsciousness, so that a spiritual being can speak through them requires an extraordinary trust. In this case the channel knows nothing about what has passed between the
Teacher who speaks through her and those who are listening until she is told by the audience or
hears a tape recording of the proceedings.

Now, through our medium, he has voice and individual stones can be brought to him to be energised, to be appreciated. When they are within his hands they tremble with delight and they continue to do so, because that energy never leaves them.

It is simple, everything that Elijah creates and shares is simplicity itself. He truly helps the beginner to understand their trade more deeply and in that way to be much more effective in what is shared with the sick.

When speaking about this book Elijah said:

Ultimately we hope that the words we give will be taught to others, so that they can begin at the beginning and learn stage by stage.

Crystal healing is infinitely simple. If you look at a famous surgeon who is successful, he uses the same technique over and over again. He is trying to perfect what he is doing, while at the same time trying to produce less pain or inconvenience for his patient, to make the aperture smaller and to create fewer lesions within the body and on the skin. He doesn't say: 'I took this appendix out with a one-inch incision; next time it will be six, to make it look much more grandiose', but this is what many want to do with crystal healing. They want a wonderful display of colours and stones in order to say: 'Just look at what I have created here!'

If you really analyse it, if one of us came along we would say: 'Take them all away and put down that one little quartz, measuring the size of a thumbnail, because it will do just as much as all those fantastic stones.' Now that is taking it a little bit far, but you know what we mean. If a stone this size works, why use one you have to carry in a sling?

Key teachings

In order to provide a context for their approach to crystals and healing some extracts of the key teachings from the Arimathean group on the soul and on the Children of Light appear as appendices.

It is not the job of this handbook to convince people about the source of the material; the material stands alone. If it resonates with your heart and furthers your understanding, then its purpose has been served. If it inspires you to learn more about the teachings as a whole, a contact address appears on page 159 for you to make further enquiries and to receive information about other books published by the Leaders Partnership.

Information about the compiler

I come from a Local Authority background where I was a senior manager in Social Services. I have an MSc in Organisational Behaviour and work as a freelance mediator and trainer.

Seven years ago I had to overcome a great deal of personal scepticism. I loved crystals, but was put off by healers who worked with the unseen and, as far as I was concerned, unseeable, intangible and slightly suspect 'new age'.

But with encouragement from the Arimathean, who could see potential within me that I could only scoff at, I enrolled on a crystal healing diploma course. My intention was to learn about crystals and leave the 'healing bit' to others.

What followed was not only a steep learning curve but also a personal transformation. I had to move from external motivation to internal inspiration and to take a leap of faith into the worlds which exist beyond the immediate and the certain and yet which were just as tangible when I opened to them. I had to learn to suspend my disbelief and self-criticism which constantly threatened to sever the link between myself and my intuition.

The college course, and much of the published information available to me, augmented, and at times conflicted with, the teachings I was receiving. Therefore, within my practice, I compared and contrasted the disparate facts and different approaches. I find the techniques and information presented here to be both powerful and safe – above all I appreciate the simplicity of the approach. I share this material with great confidence and include some personal experiences and the experience of Rosalind Pencherek, another crystal healer who has been using these techniques over some years. Rosalind is currently compiling *The Way of Diet and Health*, which contains detailed advice from the Arimathean on a range of health topics. She has kindly let me have some advance extracts which are included in this handbook.

How to approach these teachings
The purpose of this handbook is to provide practical help for individuals who wish to develop their skills in a logical and incremental way, or possibly, to complement previous training. Some of the exercises suggest that you work with another person in a 'healer – client' role but this is not meant to imply that at the end of the book you will have achieved 'healer' status. There are diploma courses available to those who wish to become fully qualified.

The approach, the techniques and the spiritual framework stem exclusively from channelled material. What this book aims to do is to put that information into a practical context by including the comments and the experiences of two crystal healers.

All the direct teachings appear in italics. In many places the plain text is taken from a direct teaching, but one that has been edited to reflect the written word and to suit the context of this handbook. Where significant editing has taken place, italics have not been used because, although the content remains intact, it is not verbatim. In some instances I have included questions and answers to provide a sense of the dialogue that takes place during the trances and hopefully to provide some answers to questions of your own. In order to retain some of the flavour of the teaching sessions I have included some text in which the Teachers go off at a tangent to the main subject heading. This is because I consider that the points that they make are interesting, almost as if they are answering questions which have had not yet formed in our minds.

11

The approach that the Teachers take is as follows:

All mankind and many souls in spirit can learn from this: to be great is to be whole – it is not that which is learned and spread among others in the sort of 'I know this, you do not' way. It is the simplicity of total knowledge, of being immersed in that which you truly love.

You have begun along a course of knowledge which has taken a million years to grow within you. At the time of Atlantis the knowledge of crystals was supreme. With the perishing of Atlantis some of the knowledge and precious commodities went to Egypt. Here they were refined, until the way of life that evolved meant that crystals were no longer valued by them.

With the coming of the Golden age the crystals will, once again, become important within the healing disciplines and therefore this journey of rediscovery which you are beginning is just that – a journey.

What I have learnt to accommodate and accept is that the information does change to reflect the needs of the Earth and of mankind, and in response to the vibrational changes that have been taking place as we have moved towards the Golden age. Elijah has reassured us that the fundamental teachings will not change, but their application might need to be refined. My own understanding is that certain changes that took place before the Millennium, and which are still continuing during 2000, have accelerated the vibration rate of the crystals, at the same time as increasing the sensitivity of the human body towards crystal energy. Therefore, I am now reviewing each of my cases to ensure that I do not simply repeat old practices without a thorough re-assessment of both client and crystals. Given the importance of this time in history, and the strength of the energetic changes, it is truly an exciting time to be involved in the reawakening of such a beautiful art.

As Appendix 1 on page 135 I have included the complete trance which Elijah gave during a crystal healing course in February 2000. Here he refers to these changes and answers questions which the students had after working through the material in this handbook over six days.

Glossary of terms
This book is based entirely on the teachings from one source and therefore some of the words and terms used have a particular meaning in the context of this handbook which may conflict with or confirm your personal understanding. In order to avoid some confusion, here is a brief explanation of some of the meanings which the Teachers apply to the following terms:

Alchemy: Originally the word was used to convey the way man could use his mind to influence matter. This was done by thought and certain incantations. Some early men – very, very few – could conjure up things using only the power of their minds. In the Middle Ages and the 16th century it was used to describe the pursuit of trying to transform base materials into precious metals. In fairy tales and Jungian psychology the process is seen in a more symbolic way: the ability to transform the suffering of experience into compassion and understanding in the crucible of the heart.

Aum: The sound of the universe. When we intone the aum it raises our energy from our lower chakras (grounding) into our higher chakras (spiritual link). When meditating we are advised to use a minimum of three aums, and a maximum of twelve; this raises our vibration levels and enables us to make contact with the spirit world.

Aura: The aura is a three-dimensional electromagnetic field that surrounds the body. It is like a candle flame; if you look closely at the wick you will see a blue shape, surrounded by a darker area that is more blue–grey in colour. Surrounding this is an oval-shaped field of energy which is primarily gold or yellow, within which there are varying degrees of colour. Beyond the flame itself is a subtle, oval-shaped energy field which produces a 'dissipating glow'.

The human aura extends on average 5–6 feet (1.5–2 m), beyond the body. The different fields within the aura relate to our physical, emotional and mental health and become progressively more subtle and diffuse. (Hence the term 'subtle bodies' which some healers use.) Every aura is as individual to a person as their fingerprints. The aura, and its relevance to healing, is described in detail on page 29.

Chakras: Subtle energy centres which are located principally in line with the spine. There are seven major chakras, each one governing a different aspect of life. An understanding of the chakras is very important to crystal healers as they form the basis of a great deal of diagnosis and treatment. They are described in detail on page 37.

Children of Light: The Children of Light are very old souls who have no further need to incarnate. They have voluntarily agreed to be born at this time in order to help the transition of humanity into the Golden age. They are highly intuitive with a deep sense of purpose and are distinguished from the rest of humankind by having no karma. There are two streams of these children; those who had their major incarnations during the time of Atlantis and those who lived important spiritual lives during the Egyptian dynasties. The eldest are currently in their late teens. For a full description read the Monograph book entitled *The Children of Light* by Father Abraham, an extract of which appears as Appendix 2 on page 146.

Christos: The Christos is the love aspect of God, the action of God the creator. The energy of the Christos was embodied within the man who was known as Yeshua and later as Jesus. The Christ refers to Yeshua's achievements, His teachings and the example He left as a signpost to the Christos.

Earthing – grounding: I use this term to indicate that a client, or healer, has an energetic connection with the earth. The healer needs to have a connection with the Christos energy, or the Earth energy within the crystals, but this also needs to be grounded in the more dense daily reality so that you can take responsibility within the healing environment. The same is true for every client; as a healer you need to ensure that they are able to take full advantage of the healing energy, and also that it is grounded, or earthed, by them in order to integrate it into their daily life. It is especially important that they are grounded, or earthed, before leaving a healing session.

Etheric counterpart: This relates to the concept of 'as above, so below'. Everything that exists on the earth plane has an etheric counterpart in the spiritual spheres. In crystal healing, from time to time, you may call on the etheric counterpart of a crystal to assist you in the healing process.

God: The creator, or creative principle. Not the God as portrayed in religion but a universal source of intelligence. In *The Way of Soul*, the Master refers to God having three principles: a creative energy – intelligence, which gave rise to God the creator. The Christos, the love aspect, and the physical embodiment of the Christos in Yeshua – the Christ. Three principles in one.

Higher Self: The total soul. Each individual soul is an aspect or particle of a Higher Self and each Higher Self contains more particles than there are cells in a human body. Not all aspects incarnate, just as a woman has the potential to conceive hundreds of children in her lifetime but may only actually give birth to two or three children. At the end of life the individualised soul returns to the Higher Self and the experiences and learning of that life are shared throughout the entire Higher Self. Once an aspect has incarnated it cannot return; each aspect or cell of the Higher Self can only incarnate once. Because of this, when a soul returns, something akin to a conference takes place where the karma is reviewed, the experiences and understanding of life are evaluated and a new aspect steps forward, with the essence of the previous life within, to take the learning forward.

Karma: 'Cause and effect', the principle that everything that you do or think creates an energy which has an effect. When the term karma is used, it is usually with reference to the lessons which the soul needs to learn in order to be able to progress both in this life and eventually through the spiritual spheres. Karma can relate to past lives, as the same lessons will be made available to the different aspects of the soul until they have been overcome.

Light stream: If the Higher Self could be seen, it would resemble a vast rainbow with the particles that comprise it organised according to the colours of that rainbow. These are called light streams – pink, amethyst, gold, silver, green and blue and all the hundreds of shades in between. Each light stream has a different learning pattern and this pattern takes an average of two to three hundred incarnations to fulfil.

Self-healing: Forming or re-forming, a healing link with the Christos, often as part of a meditation routine, which enables the revitalisation and regeneration of cells within the body, see page 51.

Shekinah: A Hebrew word meaning 'to reside' which, when chanted, connects the Christ – Christos – energy with man.

Spirit guides: Aspects of the Higher Self who have lived their lives. If invited, they can communicate the wisdom and understanding that they have accrued during meditation or trance.

Spiritual healing: Channelling the energy of the Christos, through the mind the soul and into the energy of the body; either towards a client or for self-healing purposes.

Spiritual spheres: The spheres of energy in which spirit resides. There are seven spiritual spheres surrounding the planet, the closest resembles the Earth and earthly life and each subsequent sphere progressively becomes more spiritual, colourful and attuned to spiritual advancement. The concept of 'as above, so below' applies to the spiritual spheres where all the achievements of mankind are already in existence, in what could almost be described as holographic form, because any manifestations are created through pure thought.

Subtle bodies: Another name for the various levels of the aura. Most healers work by addressing the subtle bodies which they believe contain the matrix, or blueprint, of the actual physical body.

Universal Law: The sacred laws of creation, the way things are. For example the law of balance, which implies that to be healthy and happy people need to both give and receive. If you only ever give without taking you will quite quickly become empty and have nothing more to give. The law of balance requires both; doing only one simply doesn't work.

Chapter 1

History and context

*Crystal healing establishes within the personality the
connection between Earth and God.*

The Arimathean

What is healing?

The Arimathean teaches us that all forms of healing, whether purely spiritual
or using crystals, have as their foundation the 'single cell principle' which he
describes below:

*True healing comes from within the self. The cosmos, that which creates all life,
showers healing energy within the universe and in particular throughout the
world. If this did not take place, there could be no life, for healing energy is the life
force, the spirit, which creates within mankind the ability to live.*

*When a child is born, that energy is within the single cell which comprises the
personality. From this single cell the whole of the body is manifest. From the time of
conception, healing energy is within that cell. Unfortunately, as mankind grows
and matures, the events of life begin to destroy the self-healing ability within the
cells of the body. Although initially each cell renews itself, every few hours in the
very young, every few weeks in youth and over months in later years as the body
matures, this healing energy begins to grow less within its power, so the body ages.*

*The true benefit of healing is to enable the reconstruction of cells, to deter the
ageing process and to allow humanity to remain healthy, alert and full of energy.
When you give healing to a person, the energy which flows through you to your
patient energises their cells and enables them to revitalise themselves, to have new
life within them. It is this revitalisation, and this only, which encourages health
and prevents an illness becoming terminal.*

*The mind plays a great part in the understanding of health. If an individ-
ual has great pain in their life, or great sorrow, great anxiety, then the ability to
renew and to re-energise becomes less. This can start at a very early age if the
karma of the soul denotes it. Karma plays a great part in the acceptance of healing
and in the radiation of energy which is absorbed into the body from the healer.*

*It is untrue to say that self-healing cannot be attained. It can, and is, con-
stantly. First with the renewal of the energy force which is part of life itself and then
through the determination of the individual to overcome, to prevent the debilita-
tion of the illness and allow their cells to reproduce and be re-energised. Karma
can affect this process to a great extent.*

Applying the single cell principle to healing

My approach to the single cell principle has been twofold: firstly I use it as the
underlying conceptual framework for my healing work; secondly I either use it

as an internal visualisation as I work at the crown of my client, or I include it within a visualisation with my clients at the start of the healing session. (See page 100.) During the visualisation I use a symbol to represent the single cell:

It is not easy to imagine the single cell – almost impossible to do so – so we suggest that a symbol is used, usually that of a star, sun, or moon, anything that represents life, progress and wholeness. Then when you are doing your distant healing (see page 119) or your own self-healing because of some malady, you imagine this symbol and send the healing within it, radiating truth and love and wholeness.

Later in the same teaching he continues ...

When the healing energy leaves you, it travels around the health aura of the patient. Spirit can judge exactly where in the body that energy is required; you cannot. Your patient may tell you that there is a problem with the heart, or the lungs, they may tell you they suffer from tension, or have arthritis or rheumatism, but only the soul is aware of what causes it and why it is manifest within the body. So you are healing the soul and not the individual personality. As the soul accepts that cosmic energy within itself, it then radiates into the body that which is needed.

If the soul understands that the illness is transitory, it will go fairly quickly, but if the soul has awareness of karma, the illness may be far more indwelling than transitory, and all that healers are enabled to do is bring a sense of peace and tranquillity within the mind.

Never, under any circumstances, promise that you can heal. Whatever you may feel within yourself, you cannot understand the karma of another, or understand what has brought about the illness, nor yet how long it will remain within. But you can promise a sense of peace, you can promise your compassion and a listening ear, even a shoulder upon which to cry. There is nothing magical about healing. Healing energy is within the life force of all creation.

What is crystal healing?
When you use crystals you are making a connection with the whole of the Earth energy, the ability of the Earth to heal itself, and its connection with the God force.

Crystal healing enlivens the nature of the body to its full potential. It lets the inner consciousness of the cellular structure of the body be more aware of its nature and what it is intended that it will accomplish within its life. Very often, especially if a body is beginning to age, it loses its momentum, it loses its purpose, and crystal healing helps the cellular structure to reawaken to the original purpose that was intended for that body.

What does this mean practically? It means placing crystals within the aura of a client to provoke change and self-healing. In this handbook you will find crystals are placed around the client, not on their body. (See page 96.) The change which is promoted through the power of the crystals comes from the vibration within each crystal and its resonance with the personality, the soul and the body of human beings. It is a vibration which is so pure and constant that it helps run our computers and watches.

Crystals work holistically. They do not work on the painful knee or the aching head, they work on the energy that surrounds and animates the human form – the aura. Because crystal healing works on a vibrational level it can both change established patterns of ill health, and prevent new patterns, which may be moving towards the physical form, from taking hold. It can affect our thought patterns which can create ill health or dis-ease – a sense of being ill at ease with ourselves.

The energy field furthest away from the human body (and closest to the spiritual spheres) contains or embraces patterns of ill health before they appear in the health aura. The health aura is closest to the body and is the most dense of all the layers of energy contained within the aura as a whole. Ill health, disease and emotional patterns produce an energetic response which, if you were able to see the aura, would appear as redness, 'heavier' patches of energy or 'darker' shapes.

Exercise 1

Visualising healing energy

This is an exercise from *The Way of Diet and Health* which was given by the Arimathean as a way of visualising healing energy. It can be used as a self healing – energising – routine, or as part of a crystal healing.

The purpose of this exercise is to visualise circular energy, to bring energy down and to circulate it around the body of another. For this exercise your partner can either lie or sit and you can sit either behind, or in front. You need take no action, the process is one of visualisation.

First give your partner something to concentrate on with their eyes closed, such as 'their colour'. Some people may be aware of the predominant colour within their aura, either through meditation or through information from a Spiritual Teacher, or you may have an intuitive sense of what the main colour within their aura might be. One clue can be the colours that they are wearing; often people unconsciously choose their clothes to reflect the predominant colour in their aura or to supplement a colour which is lacking.

Ask that they stay silent for the period of the exercise and agree between you a signal to indicate when the process is complete.

Start about 40 inches (1 m) above the top of the head.

Visualise golden light coming down towards them.

See it divide into two when it reaches 9 inches (22 cm) above the crown.

See two rainbows of light, one moving down the left and the other moving down the right side of the body, crossing at the feet and continuing up the other side.

When they reach the crown again, visualise the two streams of light continuing to revolve, and then moving back down and around the body alternating, as they go. Let that become faster and faster within your inner sight.

You can, if you wish, use two colours of different harmonies, deep pink – pale pink, deep green – pale green, whatever comes to the mind.

You can, if you know what it is, use the predominant colour within the aura of your partner and divide it into a paler and a deeper shade.

As it goes round like a Catherine wheel, it is cleansing, harmonising, uniting the aura with the personality of your partner.

Gradually slow it all down until it reaches a stop, over the crown chakra.

Imagine another stream of light, this time a creamy pearlescent gold, which is the colour of the Christos, coming down, moving through the chakras and into the body, filling the entire body with the Christ light.

See the revolving taking place again, this time inside. Start slowly in a clockwise direction, all around, inside the body and let it gather momentum for a moment or two. Then slow it down and bring it to a stop.

Now, here is the clever bit, do both at the same time. Visualise the double stream of colour commencing at the crown, beginning to move round the body very slowly and at the same time a stream of Christ energy entering and moving in a clockwise direction inside the body.

As you visualise, this kaleidoscope of colour begins to intermingle as the beautiful Christ energy moves outwards, linking with your partner's colour, going beyond it, still moving, still gathering up the cleansing and the energy needed within its movement.

After a moment or two allow it all to slow down and cease. Hopefully your partner will then share with you whether they experienced any sense of release or relaxation.

Ask them to explain what they felt at each stage, so that you can understand the full impact of this pattern of energy.

The larger context

It is stating the obvious to say that crystals come out of the earth, but some-times it is easy to forget their origin, and their purpose, when they appear clean, polished and shaped into the hand-sized pieces and ornaments which adorn our bodies and our homes. At the core of the Earth itself is crystal and the impact it has on our lives is explained here by the Arimathean:

We really need to take your mind back possibly two million years to when the crystal that surrounds the core of the Earth was first initiated. At that time it was purely clear, no hint of colour whatsoever. Then colour gradually came, it gradually changed and the crystal became aware of its many parts, its many functions. Within what eventually became different continents the crystal beneath each surface held a different hue. This radiated into the soil of the earth itself coming up through the many layers which compose the many hundreds and thousands of years of development.

This is one of the reasons why we advise people that it was their soul that chose where they were to be born and therefore, they should spend at least part of their lives in that area, drawing into their body the essence that it needs for its future and for their enlightenment and purpose. Few have yet been made aware of this property within crystal and the different colours mainly because people are just becoming aware of crystals, their purpose, and how they will be used in the future.

But now, unfortunately, that beautiful substance of crystal which still sur-rounds the core has been eroded, much of it has broken away from its source and has come up either through the oceans or through land. Many people now have within their collections fragments, or even larger pieces, of the original crystal core upon which the Earth was created. The energy within these pieces comes from the very beginning, the very movement of sound and echo which was within God as He breathed upon the firmament.

It is those crystals, and fragments of crystal, along with many of the minerals which form part of our world which contain healing energy and have the power within them to transform the cells within the human being. The crystal has the greatest healing power of all the semi-precious stones.

It contains deep within its heart the transforming energy of the cosmos itself. Each light refraction and fragment reflects the whole. If a large crystal should break into pieces, each piece, however small, contains the same energy, the same reflection of the universal mind as the large crystal. Each fragment has the potential to respond to an individual and provide a healing ray which will meet their needs.

At the beginning of time it was accepted that man's mind could both form and transform light and that the human mind had the power to create change. It was this natural in-built link with the cosmic mind that gave mankind the poten-tial to be able to transform and influence their reality.

You may feel that this is magic, but why should there not be magic within the world? Is it really so impossible to imagine, that one of the most ancient minerals to be found within the surface of the Earth still has this magic, and has the power to be able to help and cure man?

Crystals and their place in Atlantis

Much of what is known about crystals in the spirit spheres was learned during the Atlantean period. In fact it was the misuse of crystal power which ultimately brought down the Atlantean civilisation. The Atlanteans developed a science which was based on mental power, vibration and crystals as sources of energy. The following information is a compilation of information that has come both from the Arimathean and Elijah over a period of time, often as a comment at the beginning of a teaching session – for example when we had been caught in traffic and arrived late and full of frustration. I include it because it provides a series of images of life in Atlantis:

Although it may be difficult to comprehend, society was as well advanced as it is today with universities, places of worship and homes of great beauty. The Atlanteans were able to link their minds directly with the spiritual spheres. Spiritual Masters were able to materialise and to bring information and knowledge which enabled the civilisation to progress. There were great riches, a good government. But as people developed and became aware of 'free will' and 'freedom of expression' they began to question the need for spiritual guidance because they had the power within themselves to be able to alter their own surroundings at will.

The ability to make things materialise through the power of the mind was profound, especially amongst the priests, many of whom were alchemists. (See page 12) Crystals were their main source of power. They used crystals to power small hovercraft-type vehicles which individuals used to travel in. Even then there was a problem with the congestion of the skies and single-person vehicles were soon abandoned in favour of 2–4 person vehicles. Later the skies became so crowded that many had to revert to walking.

In Poseidonis, the last land left to the Atlanteans, there was one huge crystal known as the 'Power House'. It was kept in a temple surrounded by pillars of stone which were inlaid with different crystals. Each pillar had its direction and solar energy was drawn from it and into it.

It was the misuse of this power and the disassociation from Universal Law that led to the destruction of this continent. There was extensive flooding and a series of natural disasters. At first people fled to the highlands and continued to work and educate the tribes about the advancements in knowledge that had been made in the cities.

The destruction of Atlantis

The time when the entirety of Atlantis was one complete continent was some

150,000 years ago. The very last part, about 80,000 years ago, was the island of Poseidonis. Virtually by then there was little, if any, of Atlantis that was habitable. The island itself was sunk beneath heavy trees and the explosion of the mountain with all the lava that had poured across it. At one time the island and the mainland were divided by a small causeway. But this became impassable as the coastline of the mainland became eroded by higher and higher seas. Eventually most of the work with crystals took place on the island of Poseidonis.

Over the last 10,000 years there was even more difficulty with the energies of those that were working for the light and those that were not. Therefore, it was important that there was a complete separation as there is these days between England and Ireland. There needed to be sufficient ocean between the two so that vessels were needed to ferry people between the mainland and the island. Previously the separation had been less, similar to the distance between England and the Isle of Wight. It would have been about 80,000 years ago when the island was sunk.

About 15,000 years ago the last remaining uninhabited portions of Atlantis were just small pieces of the original country, separated by lakes and oceans .

The ability to rejuvenate the body using crystals

In one meditation I saw a young man, who is a past aspect of my Higher Self, lying on a bed of amethyst and waking up next to another young male who was dead. In a state of shock this young man picked up a crystal wand which was lying next to him and left the cave. I asked the Arimathean about this image and his answer provides some detail about how the Atlanteans were able to rejuvenate their physical bodies:

One of the the events which was prevalent at that time was the ability of man to be able to lie down in a state of near death, transform the energies within and reawaken rejuvenated and with the powerful energies within to be able to go forward for many more years of life. That transformation affected the look of the personality, perhaps 15-20 years would disappear from the body, rejuvenating the organs as well as the external appearance. So those that reached perhaps 60 or 70 within their life would be able to rejuvenate to their 40s or 50s and continue their life until they felt that once again rejuvenation was needed. A lifespan could be extended by as much as 200 years. Then the soul would return to the Higher Self and another aspect would enter life in the usual manner.

Mankind lost this ability when Atlantis itself came to the end of its age. But man is now, once more, reaching out towards this particular ability. There are those that are gently and gradually being transformed. The crystalline structure within them has the ability, through healing both from others and eventually from self-healing, to attain this within this generation of humankind. The Children of Light will have it as part of their cellular structure. As they reach middle to older age the rejuvenation will be automatic.

At this time in Earth's history it is those that realise that they have the power within, or that others could alter their structure, particularly using certain energies from crystals, that have the potential to extend their useful and functional life for quite some time. Those whose organs are already diminishing in energy will find that they are much stronger, noticeably so, so that even the medical profession will notice and comment upon it. But the potential for this transformation needs to be accepted within the self, there needs to be a recognition that this can be so and that it is not just wishful thinking.

The meditation that you entered into would have confirmed this within your mind had you been more aware of these opportunities before you meditated upon them. We interpret this as yourself, at that time, successfully communing with the energies of the amethyst that you were lying upon to rejuvenate yourself sufficiently to continue your life, while your companion was not able to do so. There are those that have truly reached the end of the time when they cannot transform themselves and their energies. They need, perhaps because of karma, to come to the end of their lives, whether still young or already much more mature.

Karma comes into all phases of life. If it is not recognised and overcome, it is not possible to rejuvenate the body and extend the useful life for possibly a further decade. It is important that the spiritual understanding within does not impose limits upon someone's ability to accept karma, relate to it and thereby overcome it in order to go forward.

Where the crystal wand is concerned, there are many kinds of wands which can be used for different purposes. Those which open a gateway and those which close it. Those which transform particular organs that have become diseased, curing the disease and allowing the organ to manifest new cells at a greater rate than is normally humanly possible.

What happened to the crystals from Atlantis?
But what of the wonderful harvest of crystal that was submerged? After a while they slept, because they were not being used. If you have crystals and you do not display them or use them either for their beauty or their working capacity, they will sleep. If they are placed away from the light temporarily, they will die and then they must be brought back to life. They cannot be used immediately because they have lost the ability to work.

It is like a human being reaching the end of a life. The soul is removed and the body disintegrates and then at some time the soul will again return, but not before it realises that it has a need for another life. It is the same with all the precious and semi-precious stones that exist. It took many thousands of years for these crystals to be rediscovered, for mankind to learn to appreciate them, at first for their unusual quality and beauty and now, more recently, for the extraordinary things which can be achieved with them.

The lessons of the past
It is worth pausing for a moment to consider the lessons of the past. For those

who question the existence of Atlantis, it is not within the remit of this book to persuade you differently. However, it is worth noting that many people who are drawn towards crystals have conflicting emotions regarding their use.

Some of this conflict may arise from subconscious memories about your use, or indeed, misuse of crystals in the past. (I have included a brief explanation on the nature of the soul, as described by the Arimathean, as Appendix 3.)

Where there is evil and the worshipping of evil, there is destruction. The law of the universe is implicit in this. Those who look within, and see light, and look outwardly and see beauty and wisdom survive these times of trial. But those that seek to gain from the empowering of others, by destroying that which others hold dear, may seem to prosper but it is transitory, eventually they will suffer and lose all.

What this handbook promotes is simplicity, a total immersion in learning and a safe but effective approach which will produce good results in a controlled environment. The Teachers often remind us that we must realise and respect the power that is within crystal energy.

The importance of this time in history

This Millennium marks the turning of the great wheel of history that fulfils a revolution each two thousand years. The transition from one astrological age to another, in this case from the Piscean to the Aquarian age, always brings challenges and opportunities and this is particularly relevant to the changes within the mineral kingdom.

The departure of the age of Pisces, with its emphasis on knowledge and scientific achievement, makes way for the dawning of the Golden age, the age of Aquarius, this brings with it a spiritual imperative; that a greater balance is achieved between the spiritual and the material. The Prophet Elijah explains:

An age does not come about simply for the same routine, the same feelings of power to generate from one generation to another, moving into the different ages, making them but one age. It is not so, it cannot be, according to Universal Law. A line must be drawn between what man wishes for in his evolution and what is ordained spiritually for humanity by the hierarchy that dwell within the spiritual spheres. Man is beginning to realise that changes must take place. He will be moved on, hurried on, in his needs and requirements because the Spiritual Teachers have so decreed. It is the same with other aspects of life, especially so with medicine.

Although the Golden age began in earnest in the year 2000, many energetic changes had already occurred – for example in 1995 I was told in a personal trance that human beings were now vibrating at a rate 1.5 times faster than in the preceding years. Those changes have been gradual and, for most of the population, they have been imperceptible.

At midnight on 31st December 1999 many of the changes which took us into the Golden age had been completed. Throughout the year 2000, and until 2004, we will continue to be affected by energetic changes. These changes will require us to update our knowledge. In 1998, for example, the received wisdom was that clear crystals benefited from the full moon. However, during that year the energy of the moon became so strong that only the opaque crystals can now sustain the energies from the full moon and the clear crystals need to be energised in the more gentle energies of the new moon.

The teachings change to reflect changes within the world, so as we start this journey of exploration we will need to adjust and reassess whether the information is still applicable. One of the intentions behind this book is to lay some basic foundations and to encourage you to develop confidence in your own intuition, so that you can constantly reassess the effectiveness of your own practice and develop an awareness of universal change which you can then relate to the changing needs of your clients.

The energy changes affect us in many ways. Our vibration rate quickens as we become more closely aligned to the vibration rate within crystals. This assists us as healers, and also means that the crystals are, once again, becoming more closely aligned to us as human beings and can therefore work holistically to create well-being and health. Elijah in June 1997 explained:

This is very important in healing. Many of you are aware that having certain forms of crystal in the area where you heal helps the energies to produce health, well-being and eventually complete healing. So the healing and medicine of the future lie within the crystals that man shares his earth with.

Scientifically man has reached his zenith in the awareness of treatments for many different illnesses. Science is finding it increasingly difficult to find new ways to treat old illnesses because many viruses have become greater than the ability of science to find an adequate cure. Doctors themselves are turning to more natural methods. A hundred or so years ago, herbs were used more frequently and with a greater understanding of their powers. This gave way to the scientific discovery, of antibiotics for example, which are no longer working to any great extent.

Crystal energy, long used in a mechanical way, is now, part of mankind's search to find a cure and is becoming a matter for scientific research. Awareness is increasing about the use of different crystal preparations.

Soon those who have knowledge and appreciation of these beautiful crystals will come into their own. They will be appreciated by the scientific fraternity for the help they will be able to give. The more knowledge you attain, the more experiments that you yourselves do, the more likely it is that the results and the cures that take place will be noted by the medical profession and they will then do tests to see whether some of the traditional medicines can be laid aside. Crystal treatments, by those qualified to give them, will supersede some of the more drastic medications that cause more damage internally than they cure.

The Children of Light

Very soon after they started speaking through their channel, the Spiritual Teachers began to talk about the Children of Light: young people who are being born whose souls have completed their round of incarnation. These souls have volunteered to return to the Earth at this time in response to the spiritual, economical, political and environmental crises that face humanity in the transition from the Piscean to the Aquarian age.

There are two streams of Children of Light, the eldest of whom are now in their late teens and early twenties, loosely referred to by the Teachers as 'Leaders' and 'Followers'. At this time the Leaders are generally younger than the Followers. They spent their most important spiritual lives at the time of Atlantis and have not incarnated since. They have no karma and have access to the knowledge of their entire Higher Selves. In the case of most of humanity this knowledge is not readily available and is mediated through spirit guides, who are generally aspects of the Higher Self of the individual. The Leaders have the most pronounced spiritual attributes; they are the visionaries whose work it will be to find positions in society where their purpose will be recognised and appreciated.

The Followers, who have had more recent incarnations, learned much of their spiritual wisdom during the Egyptian dynasties. They are the creative individuals who will take up the call of the Leaders and build the structures and systems that will reflect the vision of the Golden age. Whether Leaders or Followers, what these young people have in common is a highly intuitive and determined nature, with eyes that betray an understanding quite beyond their years. Their deep inner knowing and sense of purpose means that they do not take kindly either to direction or to discipline. On the other hand they grow and glow in the presence of love. In the second of the Monograph series, *The Children of Light,* Father Abraham said of them:

Many of the Children do indeed exhibit a rather old-fashioned, courtly behaviour. It is as if they are living in past times when the gentlemanly and lady-like behaviour was worth so much more than young people of today seem to warrant. So that is indeed a classic amongst these children. All of those who have come to us personally for our enablement to guide them – and they have ranged from between four years to about fifteen – they all had this quality. And we have also been aware through parents or grandparents describing them that they are indeed very wise children who do not behave as other children do, but seem to have an awareness of what is right and wrong at a very young age.

Many of the Children of Light spent lifetimes during the Atlantean period, when man's understanding of crystals was at its peak. As they grow and mature they will recall this knowledge and apply it to healing. To learn more about these children please see Appendix 2 page 146.

Looking into the heart of a crystal

Within the teachings both the Arimathean and Elijah have explained that crystals have a heart chakra, and it is that that resonates with mankind. They also talk about crystals having a trinity within them; soul, mind and heart and relating to the human being on all three levels.

Place a crystal in some candlelight, or daylight.

Draw close to the crystal and place your hands close but not touching, and feel the vibration within your palms moving through your (subtle) bodies until each chakra vibrates with the light that you have drawn from the crystal, the essence of all life

What do you see? What do you feel?

Which parts of your body are responding?

Which palm is the most sensitive?

When you are looking within the depths of the crystal, you are looking at one of the miracles of the world in which you live. It contains all the essence of life, which is also within you, and within everything upon your planet. However, it has a special ingredient – that spark of energy which attaches itself to the healing rays.

Elijah

Chapter 2

Light, colour and the aura

Colour lives, it is not just something which gives attraction to the plane before you. The light particles, each one is attributed to parts of the body. They vibrate to certain degrees and tones of colour.

The Arimathean

Light and colour in healing
One of the beautiful things about working with crystals is the light that they carry within them and the rainbows that attract the eye as you look at a collection of clean and well cared for stones. Their ability to refract light is remarkable. Crystals are categorised according to their refractive index and their ability to bend light and to split a single beam of white light into a myriad of colours. When you are working with crystals you are also working with light.

In 1984 the Arimathean gave a teaching on the importance of light and colour within healing.

Deprive mankind of light, and he is deprived of life. It is through the advancement of spiritual understanding during many incarnations on the Earth, or within the spiritual realms, that mankind moves towards the light. Not only in the progression itself but in the seeking of truth and by dwelling in the realms of light. This is why many healers and crystal workers refer to themselves as 'light workers'.

Once you have progressed towards the light, you are able to perceive in it all the colours of the spectrum and the many other facets of colour which the human brain finds impossible to envisage.

Much has been said of the use of light and colour in healing. Those spirit teachers who dwell among you, seeking to help and sustain you in your work, have asked that the light and colour applied in healing should come from an inward spectrum, that which is felt, rather than that which is seen. This is because of man's inability to be able to visualise true colour in all its beauty. Colour lives, it is not just something which gives attraction to the plane before you. The light particles, each one of which is attributed to a different part of the body, vibrate to certain degrees and tones of colour. For example, the liver is made up of many, many particles of light, each one different within itself. It cannot be envisaged by man, and yet those in the spirit realms who can see through man, who know man as a whole, can see each particle of light vibrating within the frame. If an organ in the body is malfunctioning, or is diseased, it is because the particles of light are no longer coordinating in the way that they should.

During healing, when hands are passed over the body, the energy of light which passes through them is able to re-harmonise the light particles, enabling all the organs to work harmoniously together.

The mind can create the disharmony, the mind with its desires and hopes. The mind can cause, and does cause, all the illness within the human structure. The anger which goes on within the brain can create disharmony between the colour particles in parts of the body, causing the disease. The only cure or help is in the hands of the healer and the mind of the Creator.

These particles of light, which dwell around you and are part of you, are so readily seen by those who live within the spiritual spheres. These souls often harmonise with healers to endeavour to ensure that the healing power is used in the right way and with the right degree of strength. They are your eyes. They enter into your mind and enable you to create the pattern of healing.

The aura

When considering the link between healing, light and colour it is important to understand how the body itself reflects light and colour. As the Arimathean has just described, we are in fact made up of many particles of light and the light that is within us and surrounds us is what makes up the aura. In 1985 the Arimathean gave the following teaching on the aura:

The aura surrounding everything within the universe is magnetic energy and vibration. The thoughts, feelings and condition of the body are all reflected in this magnetic field, causing a variation in pattern which is individual to each being.

Every aura is unique, even those of identical twins. In the spirit sphere it is as individual to us as your names are now. Where only the etheric exists, it is by the slight differences in the outline and the pattern of colours that souls recognise one another. Ultimately, on the highest sphere of existence, the rays of light become so refined that it becomes white light in which there is no reflection of colour.

From a healing point of view, if the aura can be seen or felt, and particular colours within it are seen or felt to be strong, you can judge a little bit regarding the nature or personality of those people by the strong colours that are present.

You can tell if somebody is particularly intellectual, that they consider life very seriously and work at what they are doing with an intensity, by the degree of blue. If somebody is very compassionate, very gentle within their nature, a very soft person, then it can be pink. Somebody good at balancing problems within the nature of others, very often counsellors, are green because they see both sides of a story and both sides of a nature. Gold is an intensely spiritual colour; someone who is not particularly practical, but who does have an essence, an awareness of the need of others from a spiritual perspective, they often have a high degree of gold. The purples and all the colours of the Higher Self can show an aptitude to many different things which can be done, of a spiritual and practical nature. People who are purples or amethysts have a lot of red within their blue, they are blues who have more of a spiritual mix. So you get the idea here, but actually seeing an aura is very rare. It is rather more being aware of a colour on an inner level, or taking a guess at a colour that might be predominant.

He speaks of the seven degrees of the aura which stretch out into infinity. Most people are aware of the health aura which is closest to the body and seen as a greyish outline rather like a mist, merging with the physical form.

The mental aura surrounds the health aura and this reflects the patterns of the brain, the thoughts which occur within the mind. Often the Arimathean makes a distinction between the mind (able to connect with the higher spheres) and the brain (the physical mass) but in relation to the aura he says that they are closely aligned. The emotional body reflects our feelings from moment to moment. He continues:

The emotional body changes instantaneously as your feelings change. Your thoughts are varying patterns within you and alter the vibrations. Your feelings are reflected within this part of your magnetic field. It is mainly the emotional body that others sitting near you are aware of because, as your aura spreads, the emotional body can be as far as one foot (30 cm) away from you. Anyone sitting close at hand, say within one foot, can feel their magnetic field blending with yours.

The most significant part of the aura is the spiritual energy field. This is pure gold, and spreads into infinity, reaching out into the spirit spheres where it blends with the eternal light of spirit. Those who are able to see this spiritual body soaring outwards into infinity can describe these wonderful gold rays, spreading like spires all over the world.

Looking at an aura
If you could see an aura, would you see the particles of colour that you have described coming up through the body and then blending and mixing around the body, with the chakras as the main focus?

A: Yes, that describes it quite well. Rather like a spiral, because the body is not flat and the chakras are not flat solid discs, they vibrate through the depth of the body and they interlink one with another from the top to the bottom.

Their auric value intermingles one with another which can lead to a slightly blurring effect in which none of the colours are clear cut, they merge one into another, which can be very beautiful to those who have spiritual sight.

Seeing illness in the aura
Within an aura, if illness is either present in the body or moving towards the body, that would show up as red heat or darkness. Are there other signals we should be looking out for?

A: Any inflammation provides redness and heat. Cancers appear as any shade between grey and black. If an organ in the body is virtually dead because of its cancer attachment, it can look virtually grey or black. But if there is an inflammation, say, of the kidney or the liver, then that looks blood red and very sore.

The size of the aura:
Does the size of the aura matter? Some people, in my experience, seem to hold their aura very close to their body like a protective shell. Working with crystals has appeared to expand their aura, opening it like a flower.

A: That is completely correct. You have probably heard of the expression: 'I pulled my aura closely around me like a cloak to protect me'. Now it may not be a conscious decision but people in danger, from whatever source, are inclined to automatically feel that they want to pull something around them. They retract their aura if they are under either physical or verbal abuse to protect themselves from feeling shattered by its vibration. If you were able to see the aura of someone repeatedly being verbally abused it would look as if it were wrapped around the body like a binding cloth ... this means that the person has a restricted ability to release it, to be able to reach out towards anyone, or to be able to give, or receive, love.

In other cases with a totally balanced, happy and harmonious personality, the aura can move into infinity. The infinite joy of seeing a beautiful aura vibrate into the distance, merging with the clouds, is not unknown. So the size of an aura does indeed vary between being very close to the body in defence or expansive, vibrant, healthy and beautiful through trust.

The difference between spiritual healing and crystal healing
From what you say, the vibration of love seems to be a trigger which encourages an aura to expand. Presumably this can happen with spiritual healing as much as through the use of crystals?

A: All the different forms of healing have a slight variance of meaning and vibration so that one might be more apposite at any one time than another. In general, spiritual healing is the safest to give if you are unsure of someone's personality or what they truly need. You can't go wrong with spiritual healing. With crystal healing there must be expertise, there must be knowledge of crystals, how they react to humanity. We would never give a crystal to the uninitiated and let them loose with a healing routine.

Do crystals amplify an auric colour?
You said that the crystals when laid around the body vibrate with the colour within the aura. Do they also amplify the colour?

A: If you specifically require that, yes. If it is not required, it will balance itself, harmonise itself and there will simply be a general rotation of crystal energy which will give a general lift to the person.

The colours within the aura and the impact of crystals.
Should you be choosing crystals that enhance or amplify the predominant

colour within an aura. For example, if someone needs to experience more love, would a rose quartz help them?

People have to be aware of the different qualities of crystals, what they are used for and whether the energy within them will harmonise and help the illness that is being treated. So it is rather more the energy that people need to balance them, rather than the colour. You could choose a rose quartz because it matches the deep pink within an aura, but find it does very little for the condition because the energy of the rose quartz is at a variance to the energy of that particular person. In another case, were someone has a lot deep pink within their aura, a rose quartz might provide a very powerful aid to healing.

So it is a very individual thing and for most people it is a quality they need to develop, to be able to feel the vibration and sense whether the colour and the crystal are in harmony with the personality of the client.

Q: So you might be looking to choose a crystal that has a quality that they lack, as opposed to one that they possess?

A: *That could very well be, yes.*

Q: Are you looking for a quality within a crystal that will boost the aura and align with the personality?

A: *A strengthening quality, yes.*

In *The Way of Soul* the Arimathean expands on this theme. I include the full text of his teaching and the questions which he responded to:

Light streams and crystals
As the light streams (see page 15) denote specific purposes and learning patterns I was wondering if different crystals relate to particular light streams. If they do, is it as straightforward as using rose quartz for people on the pink stream, or green crystals to relate to the green stream?

A: *It can indeed be applied in that oversimplified way for those who feel they want to begin to use crystals for health and well-being, or for strengthening, or protecting themselves. If they are aware of the light stream that predominates within their aspect, then yes, they can use those particular crystals, but they would need to programme them. This is something that must never be overlooked – that any crystal, however simple or complicated it may be, should not be used for a specific purpose unless it has been (a) divined for that purpose and (b) prepared for that use. It goes without saying that it should be cleansed, so that any energy that might have remained within it or upon it from an outside force can be removed.*

If all of this is taken into account and you decide that with a pink stream you will use a rose quartz, then you must programme that crystal to provide the best possible energy and to enable it to harmonise with your own energy. So it cannot be done – and this is the important point – it cannot be done by another person on your behalf. We have heard quite a lot of people say, 'I am going to give a certain crystal to my patient. I have programmed that crystal to help him or her with their illness'. But in fact this should never be done.

This is one of the lessons regarding crystals that all of you should take on board for the future. Give somebody a crystal, by all means, but remind them not to use it until these simple procedures have been carried out. Tell them to cleanse the crystal and then hold it to their forehead, because the strongest ray of energy for a crystal comes forth from that area of the body. Then, either send a thought towards the crystal, or speak using the voice to tell the crystal what they wish it to do. This way the crystal will definitely work with the person to whom it has been given, or who has chosen it. Later on, with more knowledge of the different crystals and their functions, people can go forward and have a wonderful variety of crystals for different purposes, but a very good way to start is to find out what your particular colour stream may be. It is not everyone who is able to tell this to another person, or for the individual to know themselves.

Q: But is it colour coordinated, if you are of the blue stream, do you use a blue crystal or if you are of the green stream, a green crystal and so on?

A: *You don't necessarily have to, but you can. It's a good place to start. As long as you feel the vibration of a crystal and it seems to relate to you. If you see one and are drawn to it, if that crystal does something to you, you can't turn away from it, you've got to have it. Or you feel it is exactly right for your child or your partner or your friend, then it is literally calling to you and you are listening to that silent little voice within it and obeying it.*

Q: But could it be calling to you for an eye complaint, or a skin disorder, and not anything to do with your light stream?

A: *Of course it could, and there again a little bit of knowledge is needed, in order to divine its purpose. We usually suggest that a pendulum is the best way* (See page 58.). *Although some people can simply relate to the crystal, talk to it and get, to their own satisfaction, an answer. Some use the palm of their hand, place it over the stone and ask it some questions. From experience they are able to interpret the different responses from the crystal as a 'yes' or 'no' answer.*

Using crystals to help us ascertain the different light streams.
One of the questions we asked Elijah was how you could use crystals to help us correctly ascertain the light stream of our clients. Here is his reply:

You have to use your psychic and spiritual ability to be able to ascertain within the aura which is the main, the most vibrant colour. This may indicate which light stream that individual stems from. Of course, the crystal that you would choose to stimulate your own memory and ability to see the energy surrounding your patients, needs to be one that you have been working with for sometime. A crystal that you have have immense trust in, and which you have dedicated to this purpose.

The memory within a crystal develops quite slowly. When you use a crystal initially, you should start afresh and blank out any ancient memories that the crystal has, which have no place within your life and what you are doing. (See page 71) We do not recommend using a crystal and making use of its original memory, because you might not be able to trust that crystal or the way in which it defines its information. It takes quite some time to build trust and to allow it to seek information from the past that is 'universal', rather than information that has developed from an individual.

Once you are reasonably sure that a particular crystal can help your own vision, your own third eye to open satisfactorily, and to give you vision regarding the aura of your client, then you can concentrate on the different areas within the aura, the different subtle bodies for example and seek out the most profound and vibrant colour that you see.

You can, if you wish, use your pendulum to ensure that you have chosen correctly, that it is indeed their light stream that you are visualising. When you have all the satisfactory information that you need, you can then proceed.

Having found this, what would you then wish to ascertain regarding the light stream and the patient?

Q: My understanding is that the light stream denotes the trend towards a particular learning pattern. If that is correct, then understanding this could help us to support our clients in a more focussed way.

E: *There are different ways advocated by the various Teachers but I myself became aware that the light streams help to provide the energy fields around the individuals and can give a good insight as to the personality and the different illnesses that the individual may suffer from throughout their life. This helps you to pinpoint the reason why that patient is suffering in the way that they are and enables you to go forward and choose the crystals which will best help them.*

For example, those that come directly from the pink light stream will often have respiratory difficulties or problems allied to respiration and arterial problems. So if you ascertain that the person is of the pink light stream, and they are having problems with breathing or they have actual heart problems or arterial problems, then you have to work accordingly to alleviate these symptoms and work towards a cure. But it will not be as easy to effect a total healing, because of the predominance of that illness, almost genetically you could say, within them. It is not as if they are simply prone to respiratory attacks.

Arthritis is predominant in the purple light stream. People who come directly through that stream will often be very prone to arthritis in different areas of the body. The degenerative form of arthritis, particularly, comes to those of the purple, mauve and the amethyst colours.

So make a study of the patients that you have and the illnesses that they come to you with. Endeavour to find their light stream and then with the aid of your pendulum, or from your experience with your crystals, you can set up a grid of the particular crystals that will help that condition.

Now, of course, you realise that if it is coming through a hereditary process such as the light stream, it is not only within their body of this life, but they have a predominance toward that problem in past lives also. Now you have a 'genetic' factor and you have to consider the impact of karma.

You have to balance these things very carefully. Often you will use trial and error to discover what will best help to relieve the problem. Is this clear enough?

Q: Very clear. I would love you to take us through the whole list of different colours but I think we have to work it out for ourselves.

E: *If we told you absolutely everything, you would not trust your judgement. But we feel we have said enough for all of you here to think, 'Ah, that's the reason for that person suffering in that way' and having realised the likelihood that they have that light stream, work on your third eye in order to be able to see it and to check that you are right. Once you can ascertain one person's aura and their vibrant colour, you can do it with all the people that you treat. It is the breakthrough on the first person that can be difficult. Whether you actually see, whether you feel it, or whether you think it, depends on you yourself and the way that you work.*

The difference between the aura and the light stream
When I work with clients I work predominately with their aura, and consider their light stream (if known) as a background indicator, in much the same way as I might view their astrological sign. The reason for this is that I can effect the colours within the aura, but not the light stream. The light stream might give me a signpost towards patterns and tendencies which help me to focus my healing sessions both on an emotional and a physical level.

What the Arimathean has explained is that people do have a number of incarnations on the same light stream, in order to ensure that a particular learning pattern is complete. Therefore, as a healer, you might find that the tendencies are either very strong and recognisable, or barely apparent. I base my healing sessions on what is visible, or requested, at the time. I tend to consider light streams more in retrospect when I am analysing a course of treatment and evaluating the success or failure of the sessions.

The aura, the meridians and crystals

What follows is a teaching from the Arimathean in January 1999 which looks at the aura, the meridians and the impact of crystals upon them.

It is the energy within the crystals that take up the vibrancy from the auric colour. When you choose crystals for healing you are not necessarily looking for those crystals that echo the colours within the aura, but to ensure that they have the opportunity to do so. The Arimathean gives the following advice:

Laying a crystal in connection with the aura, alongside the body for example, and using a crystal wand, or a pendulum, to ensure that the crystals and the aura harmonise, is of far greater benefit to the person, than trying to match up particular colours, or energy patterns, within the crystals and the aura. It would be a miracle if you found an exact match.

You can use a crystal wand to ensure that the energy within the crystals is raised or lowered so that they are moving in harmony with the meridians and with the auric colours. The healer's task is to ensure that they are all working together to enable health and well-being to emerge. However, the auric colours vary in their inherent ability to harmonise as they reflect the capacity of that individual to harmonise on many levels, especially emotional.

Crystal wands are shaped by man and usually have one rounded end and one pointed. In most, but not all wands, the energy goes through the wand towards the point. The direction of the energy flow depends on where the wand was carved from within the original piece of crystal. Its main use in crystal healing is to direct and harmonise different energies and, when used on their side, to cleanse the aura.

The way they would be used above would be to point the wand at the different crystals and draw lines between them. If the crystals are placed under the bed you can use a stirring motion to raise the energies towards the client. There is more information on the use of wands later on page 91.

Choice of crystals in relation to their colour.

Sometimes your advice is to use a '*blue crystal, any blue crystal, even if it is dyed*'. Are you saying that it is the vibration of the colour blue that the aura needs at this point in time?

A: To a very large extent, yes, you are right; that is a good premise. However, that does change as the needs of the client change and therefore, you should not use one crystal to the exclusion of others over the long term, without constantly rechecking that choice against other possibilities.

Chapter 3

The chakras and the meridians

If you could see the chakras moving about in the body, you would see the crown chakra like bursts of rocket light coming out, and zooming up fast to where it meets the Christos energy which is always flowing downward, toward humanity and toward everything living upon the Earth.

The Arimathean

So much in crystal healing links with the chakras, their position, function and colour that it is worth dealing with them in some depth. However, there is a great deal of information already available for reference so I asked the Arimathean how he sees the chakras:

They are not stagnant, or flat within the body with no life of their own, they have a lot of life of their own. We would almost use the word 'the fibrillation' of the chakras and different energy centres. They are like little star-bursts that every now and then are moving out of the body structure into the auric body. This is very important for the body itself to maintain its rhythm, to allow the changes of energy to take place and keep the healthiness and balance of all of the body, without any interference from any outside source.

Q: I'm interested in your image of a star burst, when some people describe chakras, they describe them as cones that come out from the front and back of the body. When you say 'star-burst', would that indicate that the energy flow has a central core with small bursts of energy emitting from the centre?

A: *Yes, you know how stars seem to glitter and how there appears to be little energy fields moving in and out from the centre, some of which seem to reflect the colours within that aura; it is very much like that. We don't think that 'cones' really describes them, they seem dead, and a star-burst is so alive.*

Q: Are all the chakras the same, do they all look the same?

A: *They all look the same, but they react both independently and differently. The chakras in the lower part of the body have a greater density, a greater protection around them. They are very much to do with the human self because they relate to more intense energies. They vibrate to the reds, the oranges, the terracottas, they are very emotional and very sexual. As you come up the body you are really beginning to radiate into the more sensitive spiritual energies, except for the heart. The heart is very much the pump of the human body, really keeping the body alive.*
   So you have got, we would say, four parts to the body: the very intense energies which are very slow to move, then you move up into the solar plexus which is a

faster vibration, lighter, more golden, more vibrant. Then up again into the working area of the body where everything is going at a great intensity to keep the body nourished, to keep it fit – the healthy side of the human vibration – here you get a steady pulsation, not as slow as in the lower areas, but more steady than you find around the solar plexus.

Once you move away from the heart and into the throat this is very, very sensitive to the sound of the voice, the self and the voice of others, all of which vibrate in the throat energy. As you move up into the mind, the God force resides especially in the third eye and crown. The crown chakra sends out energies quite a great distance, because the crown is moving toward the Christos in a direct manner.

Now if you could see the chakras moving about in the body, you would see the crown chakra like bursts of rocket light coming out, and zooming up fast to where it meets the Christos energy which is always flowing downward, toward humanity and toward everything living upon the Earth. The forehead and the throat have a more gentle pulsation, intense and gentle, which do not move like darts. The crown moves like a dart.

The colours of the chakras

If humanity were able to see colour in the way that spirit can, they would see this constant flow. Imagine that you are looking at the sea, watching the rays of the sun reflecting through some cloud and the reflection of the moonlight on the water, you would see all these different colours; one person might say it's 'blue' another, 'a deep green' and another that it is 'almost totally black'. At various times and because of different inputs, all of the colours of the chakras vary; none of them are static, every one of them flows and interweaves with many different qualities of colour. Sometimes they might reflect some lavender, amethyst, or very deep purple which makes the reflection of the other colours change immediately.

This is further complicated with the changes in energy as we enter the Aquarian age. Many of the colours are shifting and some of them are taking on completely different vibrations, which bring different colours with them. Therefore what you read before is not necessarily wrong; it is simply changing, especially at this point in time.

Crown chakra – connection with the Christos

This is the chakra where people communicate on a much higher level with the universe. Is is about 9 inches (22 cm) above the centre of the head. This is where the radiance enters, the opalescent light of the Christos, the golden light of the God force. The crown chakra relates specifically to the ethereal. The chakra appears as a bright light merging into a deep gold.

Around the chakra itself you have the brilliant colours of the purples, amethysts, the lighter lilac, all those shades intermingling together. As they intermingle they should be very vibrant, they should pulsate.

Some people see the chakras as flat, as colours that have no movement and no change. They do change within humanity, therefore one individual will reflect more colour than a friend or a stranger may in the same chakra. People who are spiritually developed will have a great deal of vibrancy in their higher chakra, maybe almost blinding, so that if you become aware of their auric structure it would be almost more than the human eye could stand. Sometimes if there is a spiritual function taking place which that person is involved in, the colours will sparkle and vibrate and become difficult to comprehend through natural sight.

So there isn't a set colour, it is a shade or a tone within a colour that you are aware of. But those basic colours are at the top of the person, depending upon the degree of spiritual enlightenment that they individually have developed.

Q: I know that you have said that the crown chakra will move more towards gold in line with the changes within the Earth as we move into the Golden age. Has there been a universal change?

A: *No, it's not that specific. We are moving into an age which is manifesting more light, more spirituality, a softer vibration for humankind to respond to. As they respond, as they become aware, seek more spiritual understanding and as life becomes less orientated toward the material, those people will move faster into that very gentle golden vibration, starting with the daffodil yellow and deepening as they become more spiritual.*

It is only just starting, it is rather more chaotic, but it is a good chaos, a spiritual chaos. There are still so many moving in harmony with the vibration of the world, which is more like the steady flow of a river, moving slowly towards the sea. When it gets to the sea, it creates waves and mingles with the eddies created when oceans converge from different directions. Currently you've got a mere trickle draining into the streams and the rivers, change has to be slow but steady. We hope that with the advent of the Children of Light, when people realise that they've got to move away from these negative energies into something more positive, then maybe in another several hundred years, gold will be the predominating colour.

Q: So are these the colours we should be aiming for?

A: *Accepting and beginning to absorb.*

Q: My vision as you speak is that as people become more spiritually enlightened and start opening toward the higher energies their crown chakra becomes more infused with gold is that right?

A: *That is what is happening in reality as people are getting much closer to the Christos energy which can now come far more deeply into humanity's aura than it could even ten years ago. If you have a deep red dye within water in a glass and* *you add green and gold dye you get an infusion of those colours. Although the red is still there, turning more into the magenta, it is much lighter in its hue, much more gentle. Try it, try putting some cochineal dye in some water and then pouring in different colours – perhaps the blue of a bleach bag, to try and get the different colours, drop by drop, and see the changes that take place.*

Third eye – intuition
This chakra is located in the centre of the forehead.

This chakra is also of the same vibrant shades but here you have a different yellow. It is rather more of the daffodil yellow, the gently creamy shade that is so delightful when it is experienced either by sight in flowers, or by merging with the beauty of a dedicated person who allows sympathy, understanding and love to emanate from them and toward those that are sick or in need of help. It usually goes with a very quiet and a very responsive nature. The third eye is very closely connected with intuition, that sense of being able to see, but without actual sight.

Throat chakra – communication
Although there are pulsation spots between the brow and throat, the next main chakra is situated in the throat, just above the dip between the collar bones.

This reflects the enablement of speech and the intelligence. You may say that many of the words that people speak are far from intelligent, they give voice to the emotion, they give voice to the thought. Some people are more intellectual than others, and here you might find a resonance within sound of the voice which can seem harsher when you compare it to those of a more spiritual or gentle nature, who might well have a much quieter and gentler vibration within their voice. The throat chakra is blue, the many shades of blue, so it can range from a bright harsh blue right down to a very gentle turquoise colour.

Heart chakra – love and power
This chakra is situated almost in the centre of the sternum.

The heart chakra is green, with a mixture of the blues within it, most predominately turquoise. If you were looking at it, you would see swathes of green, followed by swathes of turquoise, followed again by a deeper much harsher blue, all of which merges together like a wave, then a clear green and so forth in a repeating pattern. It is almost as if the pulse of the blood flowing through the arterial system reflects these harmonies. An intellectual person who responds rather more within the head, the brain, than with the heart will have harder, more vibrant colours. Those that truly lead with the heart have a much softer vibration, much gentler.

Q: Why is the colour pink and rose quartz so associated with the heart?

A: Pink and the energy of rose quartz relates to the emotion of the heart, whereas green relates to the mind element. Where red comes in, it has the objective of keeping the body nourished, keeping it alive. Usually the green superimposed over the red is, strangely enough, a stronger colour which allows the mind to absorb energy from other sources. It produces a gentler vibration than the really sharp, vibrant blues which are associated with a lot of intelligence and intellect. The green provides that little softness which relates rather more to the spiritual. When you use the rose quartz you introduce sensitivity, emotion, gentleness and love.

Q: So the heart has a physical, mental and emotional being?

A: Of course it has.

Q: Is that the same within every chakra?

A: Yes, this is what gives the body its relationship, every cell to each other. Every living part within that body has to have the relationship to the God force, which, remember our teachings in the Way of Soul, has the three aspects. Everything relates to these three aspects, on an inner level, an outer level and a God level. (The three aspects referred to are: The Creative Force – Intelligence, the Christos, see page 14, and Yeshua, the Christ. When I relate this to the chakras my interpretation is; the mind, the emotions and the physical.)

Q: So, a rose quartz would open the heart in an emotional sense, but would you select a different crystal, and colour, to work on its physical function?

A: We think a green stone, or a greeny-blue stone. Some of the crystals are a really beautiful greeny-blue and they almost seem to change their colours within the light. Those are ideal stones to use on the heart. Then, if you wish, you can follow it up with the golden stones to put in more of the developing energy of the Christos, of the God force into that area. If people are very non-communicative and have a great dislike of others, then all of those stones will help to make them a little gentler.

Solar plexus – emotional centre
The solar plexus chakra is situated in the centre of the body, three fingers width above the navel. Although it is not an organ as such, it is a distinct nerve plexus or junction in the autonomic nervous system. The colours within the solar plexus are predominately shades of orange and gold, often reflecting quite deep vibrant golds. Surrounding and pulsating within the solar plexus you will find apricots and peachy colours.

... this area is so very tender, resonating to the energies of fear and excitement. It is a very delicately attuned and balanced area within the body, an extremely res-

onating area emotionally. It is the merging of energies; it is the totality of all energy that merges together through the external spiral effect that we often refer to. If you imagine a person lying flat, the spiral of energy comes down through the universal spheres into the realm of matter, and that energy from the spirit spheres then merges with the kinetic energy of man as it enters the solar plexus and radiates throughout the whole body.

The Sacral chakra – sexual emotion
All the other chakras, except from the feet and the palms, follow a line in the centre of the body, with the exception of the sacral chakra which is a little to the left, as the Arimathean explains:

If you were to take a diagonal slice across the body at this point, it would be slightly left of the centre line. Like the heart that is not on the left, it is in the centre of the body, but it vibrates, and you hear it pounding more on the left. You have to visualise the body with all the organs presented front, back and middle, and not in one single dimension. They sit inside the body, if that makes sense.

Q: What colour is the sacral chakra?

It is very much of a deep peach colour but without the soft blue of a peach or an apricot fruit. The sacral is rather less vibrant, rather more solid within its colour. Very functional, often omitted. Many people who do diagrams of the aura omit it altogether, and so are we inclined to do.

Base chakra (or root chakra) – Kundalini, sexuality.
This chakra is situated in line with the pubic bone.

The base chakra is very red, vermilion. This colour becomes vibrant once the chakra has been stirred into action. But if it is not, if people are cold within their personality, if they can't show love, if they can't relax or be at one with themselves and those they love, then it can be a very harsh dull red. A red that shows no light within it, no vibrancy. But people who are full-hearted, loving and caring, then the fullness of that chakra is indeed for others to see and to have an awareness of.

Q: Does this chakra have more of a connection with the earth? Does it go down the body, through the legs to make a connection with the earth or do you see it as a star-burst, going outward?

A: It allows the body's connection with its earth. It's got the electrical energy, rather like everything revolving around the Earth and is drawn toward it, so that it doesn't just fly off into space. It connects the matter within the body to the earth.

Palm chakras – sensitivity of touch
Situated in the centre of the palms.

The small chakras in the palms of the hands radiate a different colour depending on what the individual uses their hands for. They can be colourless, a grey beige without any pink light within them, if the individual is self-absorbed, does little for others and undertakes no form of healing. By contrast the chakras in the palms of those who heal, who apply a healing touch, are a deep and quite beautiful pink, sometimes all shades of the pink merging together, according to the way the healer feels at the time.

Palms are very sensitive, very intuitive. There is a lot of power in touch, but it is softened by awareness within the body of the sensitivity of that which is being touched – whether it is to feel, or sense, an object, or whether it is a human being that you want to draw close to, or with whom you want to form a bond. It is a very important chakra but we can't really give it one definition, unless it incorporates that sensitivity of touch.

Q: It's almost physical intuition.

A: *It vibrates within the emotional bodies, there is a connection. In a way there is a connection here with all the chakras in the upper part of the body, and with the soles of the feet there is that connection below the pelvic area. If you touch with the feet you get a different sensation, but if a hand touches a foot there is a very powerful sensation, a bonding, whether it is the hand of the owner of the foot, or whether it is somebody giving reflexology or a treatment of that nature.*

In the basic healing layouts I do not place crystals either side of the palms, but I may work on them either through visualisation during the healing, or place my palm over theirs if there is a particular reason to activate these chakras. The other way of activating these chakras, if required, would be to ask the client to hold a crystal in their hands.

Chakras in the soles of the feet – connecting to the earth
Situated in the centre of the soles of the feet.

The chakras at the soles of the feet are rather strange. The fact that they contact the earth a lot, whether it is through a shoe or barefoot, means they reflect those earthy colours very greatly, the clay colours, the deep green, the misty beiges. All of these colours become vibrant within the sole chakra.

The ability to affect a person's body through the soles of the feet and the palms of the hands can be very important to the sick. If those chakras are quite lifeless the person finds it difficult to draw in light through those areas and may experience greater ill health because of the dullness and lassitude of those particular chakras.

In the basic grid layout on page 101 you will note that I also place stones either side of the knees. Behind the knees are chakras which relate to grounding and stability. They are similar in function to those within the feet. I always work on the feet and the knees in the same way, with a tendency to use the deeper and more earthy colours. By including the knees I feel that the grounding process is deeper and more stabilising than if I concentrated purely on the feet.

Q: Does the healing energy enter the body through any one particular chakra?

A: It can enter the body through any of the chakras.

The effect of crystals on the chakras
When you place crystals around the body you create a positive energy field, which unites colour, light and the different vibration rates of the stones. The body absorbs this energy through the chakras to promote self-healing.

Balancing the chakras using crystals
You can use crystals to give a chakra a boost. But the advice of the Arimathean and Elijah is not to circulate a pendulum over the chakras because the chakra system is self-balancing. Using a pendulum, especially one made of crystal, may interfere with this balance. When commenting on this book The Arimathean and Elijah's channel said that a pendulum being spun over her heart chakra had, in the past, precipitated a mild heart attack.

However, the self-balancing system may not be working efficiently and you may feel or suspect that a chakra is underperforming. Crystals, when laid around the body, can provide the energy which is needed to boost the functioning of a chakra without doing any damage.

If you feel that people are depleted because of an operation or illness in part of their body, then you can safely assume that that chakra has received a bit of a battering and you can request of your crystal that healing energy goes forth from it into the chakra. So it might alter your choice of crystal, might it not? You might feel that you need an old faithful that you can rely on, or a new crystal which would adapt to the needs of that person, or a very vibrant crystal that you could place in their energy field for a few minutes and then remove. The choice is yours, based upon your awareness of that person, their personality and their body.

Experiencing the energy flow from the chakras

You will need a pen and some paper within easy reach, as well as the pendulum which you use to work with clients. (Please refer to page 58 for clarification on pendulums and how to use them.)

Ask your partner to lie down and make sure they are comfortable. Some people may need pillows under their knees as well as their heads.

Kneel beside your partner, in a comfortable position so that you can reach the centre line of your partner's body with whichever palm is your most sensitive. You will be working 4 – 6 inches (10 – 15 cms) above your partner's body as you will be sensing the energy flow from the chakras, not touching their physical body.

Take the pendulum in your other hand and hold it at arm's length away from your partner's body. You will be using one palm to sense the energy, and the other to hold the pendulum outside of the energy field of your partner.

Starting with the crown chakra, which is about 9 inches (22 cm) above your partner's head, move your palm chakra, which is in the centre of your hand, into position above the body where you think their crown chakra is situated.

Move your palm around over the area of the chakra until your pendulum starts to rotate.

Note which way the pendulum rotates and the speed of rotation.

Consider the sensation (if any) on your palm: tingling, cold, heat, slight breeze etc.

If after a minute or so the pendulum has not moved, check your position, relax your shoulders and arms, move and soften the position you are holding. Change sides and try using the other palm above their third eye as here there is a physical indication of where that chakra is, ie in the middle of their forehead.

What you should experience is the pendulum rotating in a circular motion as you hold your other hand over the chakras. As you move down the body, chakra by chakra, the pendulum should alternate between clockwise and anticlockwise. Usually clockwise on the crown, throat, solar plexus, root and feet and anticlockwise on the others.

You may notice that the pendulum rotates at different speeds, providing an indication of the energy level within the different chakras.

Take a note of what you find, but be careful about making any definitive statements at this stage. Discuss your findings with your partner by all means, but impress on them that they should not read too much into what you found. There is no one 'right' response from the chakras, everyone is different and subject to different stresses and strains during the exercise. You are looking to see the relative degree of balance between the chakras, one with another, rather than judging them against some external standard.

(Variation on an exercise from the International College of Crystal Healing.
www.crystaltherapy.co.uk)

Working on the 'main five' chakras
Although all of the treatments are holistic, the Arimathean and Elijah have discouraged us from automatically working on all seven chakras in the trunk. Their basic layouts highlight the top five chakras, and incorporate the knees and feet to provide a flow of healing energy throughout the body, which is then grounded through the knees and feet. Their advise is not to provide a further boost to the base or sacral chakras, unless they are specifically depleted.

The relationship between the chakras and the meridians
The meridians are usually depicted in diagrams of Chinese medicine like lines on a tube map connecting different parts of the body. Here is how the Arimathean sees the meridian lines:

In our language the meridians are like an arterial system running through the body taking the energy from one chakra to another. If you look at a map you see all the different areas of the country outlined in different colours. Intermingling, linking each of the towns and the villages together are a number of arterial roads or rivers flowing from one end of the country to another. These are similar to the meridians. When you come to an interchange in the meridians it is like a reservoir into which the different streams merge and then continue on their way, having assimilated all that is necessary to complete the next stage of their journey. Each meridian provides a number of reservoirs in which the energy that flows around the body is renewed and revitalised as it moves throughout the human body. Although separate from the chakra system, they relate to it, feed it and are part of that rhythm and so cannot be separated from it.

Q: Two of the main meridians run both sides of the spinal column, and therefore either side of the chakra system. As the energy goes through the meridian, is there an exchange of energy with each chakra? Although the flow is separate, do the two relate energetically to one another?

A: Yes, rather like a bridge between one and another.

Q: Therefore when we create a healing layout based around the chakra system, (see page 101) do the meridians pick up what they need? By activating the chakras in the soles of the feet, do we create a flow up the body?

A: Definitely.

Separating off an area of the body

Is there ever a reason for separating off a meridian in a crystal healing setting?

A: If you have a very rampant cancer somewhere, especially in the lymphatic system, and it is in its volatile stage, you run the risk of carrying it throughout the body. The meridians move around the body, linking with the chakras, and forming an intricate pattern which has no beginning and no end. So, as with everything, it has a certain amount of danger and you have to accept that and try to overcome it, otherwise no healing would ever be done.

However, you can block off the particular area which houses the cancer. If you know that one of the kidneys has cancer within it, which has not yet spread, you can visualise the kidney outside of your visualisation of the arterial system and just bypass it. This is sometimes safer if you have a located cancer.

Visualisation

This answer indicates how important visualisation is as part of the healing process. As you create a healing layout you need to visualise the patterns of energy that you are creating within your mind's eye. When you point your wand to join up the crystals, visualise that the lines that you are drawing are golden strands of light. When you sit at the head of your client and focus on harnessing the Earth energy, and its connection with the God force, it is through visualising the flow of energy and colour that you stimulate a response within the aura of your client.

Q: I use celestite for cancers because it cools down the growth. Presumably if I were to use the same visualisation adding the colour of celestite, would that have a cooling effect on the whole body?

A: We feel in general that is true, very good for any inflammation of any kind. Sometimes all that a limb or joint needs to recover is rest. Reduce the swelling, remove the aggravation within the joint and perhaps the arthritis, if this is what it is, or rheumatoid arthritis within a limb, may abate and may be in remission for a long while. This crystal (celestite) has a wonderful effect of cooling, removing the inflammation and allowing rest to an area.

Chapter 4

Beginning to work with crystals

Spirit vibrates through these things, the simple things of life. The pure energies enter the Earth to the very core of its being, but only through those natural things which transfer it from place to place.

The Arimathean

The crystalline structure of man

According to the Arimathean it is the crystalline structure of the Earth, and the crystal at its core, which provides the magnetic force around which planetary life revolves. This crystalline structure is mirrored within the human body and enables us to walk upright. How I envisage this mechanism working, is that the two crystalline structures interact, one with another, their relative vibration rates interweaving together. It is this interaction that enables us to stand upright upon our revolving planet.

This structure is not present in most of the animal kingdom and therefore they tend to walk on all fours. Apparently where animals do walk upright, they have a modified structure, which enables them to attain their balance and to exhibit more intelligence than their counterparts.

The crystalline structure within the Earth was at its peak during the time of Atlantis and has slowly dimmed since then, as Elijah explains:

Every mineral within your body is also within the earth itself and within the world. There is no difference, there is no particular aspect of the body that is different from the earth itself, except in the way it looks, feels and relates, one to another – the way that man's temperament allows him to be very different in appearance to the soil, for example. But within the soil is the same mineral structure as there is within man in his flesh and that which is flowing through his blood. It is all the same, it is simply created in a different way and is seen and felt differently by human beings.

But there is also, both within the Earth and within mankind, an actual crystal energy which enables man to become part of the Earth in a way which otherwise would alienate him, would make it as difficult to walk, to live, to relate to the earth, as it is for mankind to be able to relate to any of the planets.

Let us forget for a moment about man's inability to breathe if he was on a planet – say Mars – where it would freeze his blood so that he could not animate himself, could not actually live. He would not be able to use any of the things that grow within the outer surface of Mars to feed himself and there is no oxygen for him to be able to breathe, to pump his heart. It is literally an alien structure, but the Earth is not, because when mankind was created, he was indeed created of the Earth, he was part of the Earth and has remained so, even though his body has become more refined over the millions of years.

A crystal is part of the Earth. A crystal was originally pure running water, solidified through the freezing cold conditions and allowed to remain in that form after the earth began to warm up, because it contains within it a mineral which allows that solidity to remain. Man is very largely liquid, but he is not running all over the place, his body does not melt, it remains solidified because there are components within it which ensure this. We do not wish to go into a great deal of detail regarding chemistry, because if we do this it will be of no use whatsoever for the book, so we are keeping it as easy as possible for everybody to understand.

Q: It sounds as if man is more closely aligned to the crystalline structure of the Earth than the animal kingdom?

A: *That is so, and there is of course the level of intelligence. There is an intelligence within all crystals which relate one to another and can be encouraged to relate to humanity as well, so that you build up a rapport with a crystal that you are constantly using for a purpose. So in its own intelligent way it understands what it is to be used for, how and when. So it is the same within mankind. There are different levels of intelligence which can be used, which come virtually from the hierarchy, the ancestors.*

An animal fulfils its potential on a more limited scale. As you have different forms of crystal in your home that you use for different purposes, knowing that one has much more energy, much more power or ability – whether it is to heal, whether to make safe, whether to radiate beauty – so also does that which adheres within a man or animal. There is the same ability up to a point or a particular quantum factor or energy within its structure.

The molecular structure of crystals

To try and describe the actual composition of different crystals is very difficult as there are so many millions of stones. Even if you have two crystals taken from the same place, there will be different energies within them according to where they have been resting, which part of the world they have been taken to and many other factors. The Arimathean explains:

So much depends upon sensation, an inner awareness of the quality of a particular crystal. There is nothing that is absolutely structured for one use or another. It is what scientists refer to as that 'x factor', which is like the soul to man. When scientists are trying to derive a God force or a soul within humankind, they fall short because they can only see the molecular structure and all that is defined there. The definition of the soul quality cannot ever be defined. It is virtually the same with crystals; they are living structures, they have a relationship to one another and a relationship to everything around them.

They were the centre force of the Earth when it was created. It was that structure to which everything else adhered and continues to adhere. So it is like the soul in mankind that is the centre of humanity. Without it the structure falls apart, the molecules cease to adhere together and perform their function, the soul returns to its source, the spirit world, and the body falls apart and decays. It is the same with crystals, because they have the ice-like rigid structure, that inner essence, that inner soul. You can crush them into tiny pieces and each fragment will still retain its original capacity.

Q: Therefore choosing which crystal to buy must be an emotional choice?

A: *Absolutely. It is the emotions of the receiver, the purchaser, that creates a demand towards that crystal, and that interaction defines its function.*

How crystals relate with the spirit world

I include this extract from a teaching by the Arimathean to try and put into context what happens when you are healing with crystals. If you come from a spiritual healing discipline, then you will appreciate the fact that you are indeed harnessing energies beyond yourself and that this can only be done by laying the ego and the personality aside. The harder you try, the less the energies flow, and so it is with crystal healing, not only because you as a healer need to provide a pure and clear channel, but because the crystals have their own relationship with the spirit world as the Arimathean explains:

The light which comes from nature is depicted by the crystal. The mind of the crystal is universal; it does have a mind, energy and knowledge. We (the spirit world) use the crystal to direct energy to those we feel are lacking. We use the spiral surrounding the crystal to negate the evil which could come in close proximity to where you dwell and where the crystal rests.

It is not our power, for we have none. It is the power of light reflected within these stones which surround you in your habitat, healing sanctuaries and places of living. We vibrate through these things, the simple things of life. The pure energies enter the earth to the very core of its being, but only through those natural things which transfer it from place to place. The rocks and stones, which form part of your nature, parks and places where you pray and worship are also energy sources and reflect light to and from the universe.

Establishing a strong link

One of the most important components when working with crystals is to establish a good link with the spirit realms, your 'guides', 'teachers' or your 'intuition'. It is in this 'meditative state' that you will receive guidance and be able to fully reflect upon, and discriminate between, the information which you have been getting from different sources. You will find that there is no shortage of information available, including this handbook, and it is important to explore all avenues. Do be guided by your intuition and sense of discernment.

Meditation

The form of meditation that is recommended by the Arimathean is simple, requires very little time and has quite profound effects. The best time to do it is immediately after waking up:

Sit quietly and comfortably in a chair and light a candle.

Spend a while gazing into the flame; in particular be aware of the golden light that the flame casts.

Close your eyes and imagine that golden light expanding and enveloping you. Imagine it entering your body through the top of your head and feel it filling your body.

Then open to whatever comes through – sensations, words, images, sounds. In the same way as we all experience life differently, so we will vary in the way in which we relate to the spirit world.

You may wish to record your thoughts and visualisations on a tape recorder at the time rather than relying on your memory and making notes after the event.

One of the techniques which the Arimathean suggests is to use an affirmation as part of your meditation. One that he recommends quite frequently is:

I am that I am, therefore I am whole.

Repeat the affirmation several times and give thanks.

Gently open your eyes and note any information, images or realisations that you may have received.

Self-healing

From time to time the Arimathean refers to self-healing crystals. These crystals are used within a simple self-healing process, which is effectively an extension of the mediation technique above. By holding a clear quartz crystal which is double terminated, see page 92, dedicated for personal self-healing, and completing the first three steps of the meditation you will be following his self-healing routine. The key difference is that your visualisation should include the image of the golden light touching each cell within your body and bringing with it vitality and health. You can, if you wish, point your crystal towards your heart chakra to initiate the start of the self-healing, but then relax and hold the crystal with one point towards the chakra of the palm you find the most sensitive (usually the left hand).

This should take a few minutes each day and can precede the meditation, but it is different; once you have completed the self-healing, then you would place that crystal down and pick up the crystal that you use for meditation. Elijah has recently advised that you will know when the process is complete when you find that you have moved your crystal from your left hand into your right (see page 144).

The crystal that is recommended for self-healing is a double terminated Brazilian quartz, as clear as possible; the crystals recommended for meditation tend to be cloudier, and often from Madagascar.

Why include an affirmation?
The purpose of affirmations is to create a positive attitude towards the future as the reality of tomorrow is created by the attitudes and choices of today. The principle behind them is that like attracts like. If your demeanour is one that is positive and confident then you are more likely to attract success than if you present yourself as fearful and anxious. The first step is an internal one. Affirmations have the potential to transform the negative cycles of fear and self-doubt into a positive stream of energy that is vibrant and purposeful, and which creates an inner sense of anticipation and achievement.

Affirmations have the effect of drawing positive vibrations into your aura, which aligns you with the universal energy, which is inexhaustible and positive. In effect you form a connection with the Divine; this can create a sense of peace and contentment, and enables you to connect with your own internal power and sense of purpose. Affirmations are one way of guiding our imagination towards the best in ourselves.

Inspiration or imagination?
One of the questions which bother most people at some time is whether the information that they get through meditation is imagination or inspiration. Personally, I find the best way is to record everything and then to look back over it after a period of time and decide what you wish to retain and what you will disregard. You may be surprised at some of the words and the insights that you have recorded. If there is a sense of 'Did I really write this?' then perhaps you are indeed receiving inspiration from your Higher Self or your guides. Imagination is like a cinema screen; the images and ideas that flicker across it can just as easily be from spirit as from our personal history.

Grounding yourself
When I heal I find there are three points at which I ground myself, or at least pause and consider whether I feel grounded. Before my client arrives, having set up the space, I take a few moments to ground myself, to review their

Grounding yourself

When working with crystals it is important to be able to connect to spiritual energy without necessarily undertaking a full meditation. You will find your own way of achieving this, but here are some basic guidelines:

Relax and concentrate on your breathing.

Have both feet on the ground.

Allow the energy to enter through your crown chakra.

Sense the energy leaving through the soles of your feet.

Note how you experience any changes in energy.

When healing you may wish to use the affirmation:

'I know the God within.'

notes and to see if I can envisage colours or crystals which they might need. After they arrive I discuss their needs with them, reassess any information which I may have received, check that I feel grounded and then choose the crystals. After the client has settled, I talk them through a visualisation to relax them (page 100), move to one side, close my eyes and ground myself by silently repeating my affirmation, before laying down the crystals.

The Arimathean and Elijah would both say that when you work as a healer you should do it separately from other more secular work. In practice this has not always been possible for me and I have found myself rushing to appointments. This tends to make me fearful that I will not be able to make a strong connection and will let my client down. I have come to trust that if I calm and ground myself and say the affirmation the crystals will do the rest. If I allow myself to remain worried and fearful then I disconnect myself from my intuition. In effect I have learnt to give myself a break but promise myself I will do better next time.

Choosing crystals

When the Teachers talk about the molecular structure of crystals, they emphasise the relationship between crystals and mankind. Choosing crystals is often more about feelings than rational decisions.

You may decide to go out to buy a 'healing' crystal or a 'protective' crystal or to buy one because it is your 'birth stone'. Sometimes it will be the sheer beauty of the crystal which will shine and attract you. Whatever your purpose in seeking crystals, do trust your intuition as much as possible. If you feel a sudden attraction to one crystal or an aversion to another, listen to your inner feelings. Often it is your Higher Self which is responding and trying to inform your actions.

As you work you will discover for yourself how stones attract you. It may be a tingling in the palms, a shining crystal, a response in your heart or a sound in your inner ear, because crystals vibrate to certain tones.

For some it will be obvious what is directing you; for others it may be more subtle and all you know is that you have a liking or an aversion but cannot explain why. The most difficult part of this path is trusting that inner sense. The energy changes are so subtle that they are often easy to dismiss as imagination. What guides me is my heart response. Often after seeing a particular crystal there is no alternative except to get out the cheque book, or credit card, and buy it.

Exercise 4

Selecting crystals

These two exercises are designed to evoke:

a sensitivity to crystals which will increase over time

an understanding of how you personally select stones

a sensitivity to how different crystals relate to parts of the body.

Take a collection of crystals, different shapes, sizes and colours. With your eyes closed, hold each of your palms in turn over the collection of stones and pick up the stones which you feel attracted to.

Notice which palm is the most sensitive.

Working through the selected stones one by one note, if you can, where the crystal affects you. Which part of your body responds to this particular stone?

As you pick up the different shapes, note down the different experiences that you have. Does a point have a greater impact on your palm than a tumblestone? Does a pyramid differ from a sphere?

You may well find one palm more sensitive than the other. You may be attracted by the sight or the feel of a crystal. You might experience a 'pull' in your heart chakra when seeing one particular crystal. Crystals often make a connection with the heart of human beings, so do not be surprised if it is your heart that responds.

Using a larger crystal to assist you

It is important, at this early stage, not to feel discouraged if you do not feel strong or clear sensations. You are working to develop your intuition and connection with the crystals. This can evoke some self-doubt, especially when books and teachers seem to expect you to trust and discriminate between sensations which are very subtle and ethereal. In order to magnify the impact of different crystals on the body try using a larger crystal that has been programmed for healing (an established crystal – see below) to assist you. Elijah once gave us the following exercise:

We wish to assess your reaction through a smaller crystal to the large one. We simply wish you to be aware of the intensity, or otherwise, of the referred energy to and from the large crystal, which will enter through your crown chakra into your body.

Take your small hand-held crystal and hold it a few centimetres away from the larger crystal. Close your eyes and monitor any changes you experience or sensations which you feel. Note where they are, their intensity and if you feel uncomfortable.

Try with different small crystals and see if your reaction varies.

Do cleanse your small stones after this exercise, before using them for any other purpose.

We found we were able to identify the purpose of the small crystals more easily, because their impact on us physically, or emotionally, had been heightened by the energy of the large crystal.

Remember not to store your small stones in close proximity to the larger crystals. Large crystals can drain the energy from the smaller ones.

Working with an established crystal

If you hold your hands around an established crystal and then around a new crystal that has no particular purpose, you will notice that their intensity and vibration levels differ from each other. You could try holding your smaller stones towards a large established crystal and see if it elicits a different response than a newer stone Elijah explains:

Established crystals, such as those that are used in healing practices, develop an understanding of their task and, provided they are well cared for, their vibration level will be strong and consistent.

The soul structure within crystals
In preparation for the work that I did for my diploma on the levels of healing (page 113) the Arimathean described the soul structure within crystals. He relates this soul structure to that within human beings which is described briefly in Appendix 3 (page 149). His explanation is as follows:

There is an essence of soul within crystals – it is the same principle as within humanity. The entire crystal – say a rose quartz, the earthly embodiment of rose quartz – all share a Higher Self – a total soul. Each fragment, each part of the rose quartz family, once it is bought into use, has the knowledge of the Higher Self within it. That knowledge helps it to relate to the person who is in need, and in light of any karma, to sort out which particular crystal should work with that person. So it is a very similar structure to that within humanity.

Q: Does the soul of the crystal relate to the personality, or soul to soul?

A: *It is again the same as with human beings. How would you say you relate to others, to their soul or their personality?*

Q: Both I suppose.

A: *Then it is the same; what you find within humanity is echoed within the crystal life upon the earth.*

Q: This relates to choosing a crystal. A celestite might be good for cancer, but may not be the appropriate choice for a particular personality.

A: *Exactly, this is why your pendulum is vital.*

Q: So, as a healer are you relating to the energy within the personality, as well as the properties within a particular stone?

A: *Indeed so.*

Masculine and feminine energies in crystals
When choosing crystals Rosalind had a sense of some being 'male' and some 'female' in their energy patterns and asked Elijah if this could be the case:

We would say so. It is possible with crystals, most definitely. Some crystals have a predominating feminine energy which, should you try to use them for a purpose that needs male strength, would not be successful. You might even fracture the crystal. So this is something else to look out for when you are treating people or when you are choosing a crystal for a particular purpose in your home.

Q: I have heard that clear quartz is feminine and cloudy quartz is masculine.

E: *That is so.*

During the preparation of the book there was a question raised about whether we had got them the wrong way round as clear quartz is so often viewed as masculine. So I checked with the Arimathean:

A: *No, it is considered that the cloudy quartz has the masculine energy because it is much denser and stronger. It is more powerful and can affect many different problems. The clear quartz is more fragile and can be easily broken, but it also has that clarity which is more prevalent in women than it is in men. Men find it very difficult to see any issue with absolute clarity. Most men are inclined to think long and hard around a problem, become very logical and rely upon their life's experience, whereas women use their intuition. So to us, there is a great difference between the cloudy and the clear, and the clear is most definitely the feminine aspect of a crystal.*

In an earlier teaching session with Elijah a question was asked about whether rose quartz and calcite are feminine, and quartz more masculine. He replied:

E: *Rubies and all stones that have a definite deep red or black tinge could generally be considered masculine. So can the blue stones, the very clear ones may be feminine, or a mixture of both, but the cloudy blue stones tend to be more masculine because they have a direct purpose and are very strong in their energy. Generally green is more of a feminine energy. You are correct that the clear quartz, especially the sparkly quartz, is feminine.*

You will notice that the more you develop both your interest and your ability, the more you will begin to consider the possibility of different elements within your crystals. They will begin, in a way, to talk to you and as they do this you will respond. Maybe not instantly, but it will give you food for thought, and perhaps the next time you decide to use that stone in your work, the thought will reverberate again and then you will give true consideration towards it.

Most of the more masculine stones can be used to generate energy that will protect. They can also be used if you ever have to dispel difficult energies away from a client, especially if you feel that they may have some kind of – how can we put this? – degenerative energy within them, or where some energy from the spirit world may be endeavouring to prevent your client from living their lives in line with their soul's purpose. Anything of a protective nature is an ideal use for the more masculine stones.

How to work with different pendulums

Elijah teaches that the use of a pendulum is an important adjunct to our practice. It can assist in confirming and reinforcing the instinctive choices that have already been made. Elijah and the Arimathean advise us to work with two separate pendulums: one that will assist us in choosing crystals, and one which will help in working with our clients. In line with all the other advice on using crystals for a single purpose, each pendulum should be dedicated for one use, although the techniques for using them are the same.

Some of you will be familiar with working with pendulums in other healing environments. This exercise is designed for crystal pendulums, the type recommended for crystal healing. You can use either the shaped pendulums available from most retail outlets or those which are made from a natural point, polished and mounted in silver or gold.

When working with a crystal pendulum please ensure that it has been adequately cleansed, programmed or dedicated and is ready for use. If the pendulum revolves in the opposite direction to its normal pattern then it is showing you that it is not ready to work at this time.

If you are working with a pendulum for the first time, you need to become familiar with how it answers questions. Basic pointers are:

Phrase your questions to cover one point and ask the question in such a way as to invite a 'yes – no' answer.

Work with your pendulum to establish how it responds. Most pendulums reply 'yes' with a clockwise motion and 'no' anti-clockwise, but not all, I have a smoky that rotates in the reverse order to my clear quartz.

Use only one pendulum for working with crystals. If you use a pendulum for other reasons, then use a separate one for each task.

The basic uses of the different pendulums

Use your pendulum dedicated to helping you choose crystals ('crystal pendulum') to:

Confirm the choice of a particular crystal, or group of crystals.

Check whether a new stone has a particular purpose.

Check the energy levels within the stones, see page 69.

Check whether all the stones you have chosen will work in harmony with one another.

Check whether a stone which the client wishes to hold, or wear, will conflict with the crystals you have chosen for a healing pattern.

Check the country of origin of a newly purchased stone.

Sample dedication:

'Help me to choose my crystals well, those best suited for the task, energised and able to work in harmony one with another.'

Use the pendulum dedicated to healing clients ('people pendulum') to:

Check whether you need to concentrate on, or isolate part of, their body.

Check out a plan of action that you might be considering based on the symptoms that they have described.

Check out whether one of their chakras is out of balance. (Using your palm chakra over their body, not your pendulum. See page 45.)

Check in with a client prior to a distant healing (see page 121). You might check, for example, if the client is ready for the healing, or perhaps in need of a particular colour. Try just letting the pendulum rotate while you visualise different colours encircling them and see if you get a strong response. If you do, try visualising that colour being enhanced through the two crystals and encircling your client.

Sample dedication:

'Give me the information I need to be able to meet the needs of my clients in the best way possible.'

How to read the response of the pendulums

What you are reading is the direction and the speed of the rotation. The direction indicates 'yes' or 'no' and the speed indicates the amount of congruence between the question that you are asking and the energetic response for that particular person or from a stone. When you are working with your crystal pendulum it is indicating both 'how right you are', and the energy level within the crystals themselves. If you hold your crystal pendulum over a stone it will rotate in tune with the energy level of the stone, regardless of whether you ask a specific question. Elijah explains:

We prefer the intuitive feeling regarding the response of the pendulum. If it is rather laggardly in starting to move, as if it is hesitating, trying to work out the response from the crystal, then that should give you your first intuitive feeling that all is not quite well. Possibly it then begins to turn, quite slowly over that crystal, whereas with another crystal it will tremble and turn quite quickly. That crystal is telling you something and so is the pendulum. We do prefer this, but if you like to speak to them, that is perfectly in order because they can get used to being spoken to. You can choose your own way of working with them.

Speaking to crystals

While we speak of talking to crystals, we know that many people talk to plants and this is not as foolish as you might think it is, because plants react to vibration and the voice is a vibration. So if you encourage your plants to flower, to remain fresh longer even when they are cut, you are not being foolish, because your voice alters whenever you speak to a plant, a pet, or a human being and your plants do react.

It is the same with your crystals. Try a little experiment; get a crystal that you have not used for a long while. Hold the pendulum over it saying and thinking nothing. Try and concentrate on something completely different and just hold the pendulum over the crystal. Wait and see what happens. You will probably find that the pendulum is disinterested, it is not much bothered with that crystal because it has not been used and the crystal is probably not feeling very loved.

Now, talk to the crystal, hold it, stroke it, behave to it as though it were a young child. Then use the pendulum and you will see what a difference that little contact, that little emotion has created.

Using the pendulum to select crystals for healing sessions
This process involves three stages: matching the crystals to the person and their condition; ensuring the chosen crystals can work together; and working out the placement of the crystals. When choosing crystals ensure that you have enough space around each crystal, or set of crystals, to keep the different energies separate from one another.

Matching the crystals and the person
I always ask about more than one set or type of crystal, and do not take the first 'yes' answer, but compare the answer for that group against at least one alternative. I feel reassured when crystals have been ruled 'out' as well as 'in'.

I tend to minimise the number of different types of crystal that I use, but if the client has presented with a particular request; 'could you work on my lower back' for example, I will match a set of crystals for the chakras, and then a stone which I will place under the bed for the lower back. I always choose each crystal individually.

Checking out that the stones can work together
Once I know the combination of the stones I ask whether they can work together. I check each crystal by rotating the pendulum over it as I move it into the group, and then I check that the different groups can work together. For example, if you take the basic grid on page 101, I would check out the individual stones for the chakras as one group, then the protective stones as a group, and then the two together.

If, as in the example above, I also intend to use a single stone for a specific purpose then I check that that stone can work with all the others that I have just selected.

Placement
I tend to choose the individual crystals, and their placement next to the different chakras, by eye but I use my pendulum to confirm my intuition. For example, if I have selected one piece of gold calcite and six pieces of green calcite, I would check the placement of the gold calcite with my pendulum. I might have thought 'gold for the third eye', but will ask my pendulum whether the crown or the third eye would be the best choice. I know that Rosalind uses her pendulum to confirm the placement of each stone.

Working with the pendulum to assist with clients
During healing sessions, if the person has mentioned a specific problem, or if I find myself wondering about a particular area of the body, I use the pendulum to confirm whether there are any patches of heat within their aura. I use my left palm to scan the body about 9 inches (22 mm) above the person, and hold my pendulum away from their body, in my right hand. A change in rotation,

or a slowing down in the spin, would indicate a difference in the aura, and as a result I might use my hands to bring some additional healing to that area.

For distant healing I allow the pendulum to start rotating as I visualise the person in question, and then consider each of their chakras, and the corresponding parts of their body, to see if the pendulum reverses its order of rotation. This gives me an indication of whether I need to focus additional energy into that particular area.

After a crystal healing course that followed the contents of this handbook Elijah was questioned about whether healers really needed to use a pendulum:

E: If you want accuracy, yes, but don't use it for everything. Don't ask a pendulum if you should go shopping, or whether you should go by train or bus, that is not the reason for it. Crystal pendulums are tuned to a vibration that works with stones, so if you are using a pendulum in that way, you are using it correctly. Until you are absolutely sure that your mind is adequately tuned into the crystals you are using, that you can pick up their response and know for sure what it is they are telling you, you will need to verify it with a well-cleansed and good pendulum.

The full teaching appears in Appendix 1 page 135.

Chapter 5

Getting the best from your crystals

Part of the beauty of many very small stones is the total clarity within them.
The larger stones are more inclined to show energy patterns which adjust
and alter according to surroundings, because there is a greater
energy flow over the surface of a larger stone.

The Arimathean

In my experience, some healers prefer rough stones, while others prefer polished. Those that choose the rough crystals believe that polishing diminishes their healing potential.

Using the polished or moulded crystals
The Arimathean has often guided us towards using the tumbled and polished stones because they give the greatest protection:

... they contain the deep colouration from the apex, the vital part of the crystal. It is this which is taken, ground, moulded and polished.

Q: Are some tumblestones reconstituted and moulded, rather than chips off larger stones which have been polished?

A: *Sometimes yes, they can be lots of little pieces gathered together, put into a bowl, crushed down, then made into varying sizes and polished.*

Q: Is that how crystal balls and spheres are formed?

A: *Yes, sometimes it is the inferior parts of the crystal that have been used – let us take an amethyst – it is often the very white, milky part of the crystal which is ground down. And yet it is the coloured part of the amethyst, that which has grown from the base, which has much more energy, light, power and healing ability. If these milky parts are moulded into a stone, it neither has the clear light nor the energy within it that smaller pieces of the dark amethyst would contain if they had been moulded.*
If there is a mixture between the two, when the ball is complete, it has a very dark density, sometimes almost a dullness, but it begins to separate within the ball itself. That separation once it is in contact with light, or with sunshine, begins to break all the way around, sometimes developing a crack, but if it doesn't do this you can still see through the ball and you can see both the light and the darker areas. The light areas produce the rainbows, the windows within the ball and the dark areas remain dense, but it is the amount of deep amethyst which denotes the healing ability of an amethyst crystal ball. Is this clear?

Q: What I hear you say is that the dark colour has the most healing potential.

A: *That is so.*

Q: Is that different for rose quartz where you have advised us that the lighter stones are best for healing?

A: *Yes, because the rose quartz starts off its life as a clear quartz. It obtains its colour from minerals within the water which drips upon it or in which it grows.*

I always use small tumblestones within my healing layouts. Some people feel that they need rough crystals, single points or expensive polished stones in their healing kit, but as you can see from this next teaching from the Arimathean the small and inexpensive stones are invaluable. In the first paragraph he is discussing a rough piece of emerald. The remaining text is more general:

In general the coarse stones, as we call them, those that have not been refined in any way for a specific use, do not have as much clear energy as those which have been refined, polished or set. There are certain more precious stones that do not have a quality within them which is suitable for healing, meditation or any other work that crystals do. If fashioned into a pendant and worn in this way this emerald would give energy, especially to those who are of the green light stream. Certainly it would be a beautiful pendant and it would have more power within it through being made into such a pendant than it does in its rough, raw state.

Part of the beauty of many very small stones is the total clarity within them. The larger stones are more inclined to show energy patterns which adjust and alter according to surroundings, because there is a greater energy flow over the surface of a larger stone. The very small ones are inclined to vibrate on a single note, which means that the breakdown of energies within them is not so profound.

You want to choose stones that are taken from as close to the apex as possible, avoiding the very pale opaque stones, unless the stone itself is of a very light variety. Clear crystals which are moulded and polished have no loss of energy. It is the energy within the collective growth which is incorporated into the smaller shape unless, of course, the tumblestones have been formed entirely from the base where there is less energy. Most tumblestones contain a mixture of material which produces a stone which has the strength provided by the denser matter from the base combined with the energy in the material taken from the apex.

Those who ignore the polished smaller stones are foolish not to experiment with them. They make excellent protective stones, and the smaller sizes can be easily carried about the body*.

---

*Please wrap them in a little silk or velvet and do not let them jangle around amongst your loose change. Remember they, too, need regular cleansing, energising and access to the moonlight.

The importance of where stones are mined

Elijah has often mentioned how the stones which are mined from under water have a particular healing ability:

The natural healing crystals, the very clear crystals, are mined from beneath the ocean or within it. Many of the caves from which crystals are gathered are beneath the water's surface. But, we can hear you ask, if the levels of the oceans become lower and these caves become part of the dry land, are they still predominantly healing crystals or do they change their nature because they then become acquainted with other energies? The answer to this is 'yes'. There are qualities within those crystals that have matured in the water which are lost if they remain on land for any great period of time.

So what, you may ask, happens to these crystals that you yourselves have gathered. How long have they been in the shops before you buy them? How long while they are in your custody will they remain as healing crystals? All very relevant questions, but we do talk here in hundreds of years, not about the short space of time that you yourselves will be using them, unless by sheer misfortune you have been informed incorrectly about the genesis of any particular crystal.

Consider the truth of what you have been told. You will then need to find out by trial and error whether a crystal responds to healing energy or is more suitable to be protective or whatever other purpose you wish to place upon it.

Using stones from the same country

The understanding that our Teachers have of the different energies and vibrations within the stones encourages me to be very careful about mixing stones from different countries:

A: Generally speaking we suggest that you choose crystals from the same country, balanced in size, for use in any pattern. This does not leave the user open to misuse. Certain energies can indeed inhibit the healing pattern within a patient. They can conflict with the energies that the patient emits. Even those who have studied crystal energy very deeply do not always accept that the vibrations within personalities are very important when mixed with the energies within the crystals. This is why in all cases we promote simplicity.

Certainly in the beginning I would suggest that you stick to this as a cardinal rule. This does present some difficulties, as not all the dealers can tell you where the crystals have been mined. Many can say where they were purchased from, but you do have to remember to ask (and make a note) at the time of purchase. Your pendulum can help you ascertain a country of origin, but only in reality if you know all the potential sources and can list them to give the pendulum the full list of options.

Some crystals are mined from limited areas, making it difficult to create a grid from that area alone. However, you can use your pendulum to check for harmony within the stones so you can use stones at different points in the healing to prevent them interacting negatively with one another.

Keeping stones for a single purpose
One of the main components of this particular teaching is that stones respond better and are more able to self-cleanse if they are kept for a specific purpose. The vibrations required for meditation are different than those required for healing and the stone needs to modulate its vibrations in line with the requests being made of it.

If, for example, you use a crystal for clarity of mind when meditating, leave it solely for that purpose. Do not use it for energising, or protection, or to carry around with you, because then it will need to exert a protective influence which can confuse its molecules. Leave the meditation stone where you normally meditate, or have your moment of reflection. If it is on your person, it will have to constantly adjust to the different variations of climate and areas of need within yourself, and then you will find its crystal clarity will gradually depart.

Keeping stones for specific illnesses
In general, when you have particular stones that you feel you need to use for a particular illness, or indeed particular clients, do ensure that you keep them separate and do test them regularly for their strength.

I have a number of stones that have particular purposes: healing broken bones, digestive difficulties, HIV or AIDS. Because their vibration level is aligned to that particular condition and I have programmed them, I use them solely for that condition, cleanse them thoroughly after each use and keep them separate from my other more general healing stones.

The initial test I used was to ask my pendulum if the stone had a particular purpose and then, by process of elimination, worked through the possibilities. One of the stones I purchased in my local market for a few pounds contained a great deal of information about nutrition and had been used for that purpose in the past.

Of course, one crystal can be used for many things, but it would be like using one universal medicine to try and cure many different illnesses. It cannot be done. You might use an aspirin to help many people who are in pain but they would need different kinds of painkiller depending on the type of pain, and their individual needs and sensitivities.

Use your intuition. If you have chosen specific crystals for, say, a patient who has muscular problems and after two or three healing sessions there is little or no improvement, or even that the muscle tension is worse, do look at the crystal.

Personally I would advise that you use your pendulum to check. If your choice of stone is wrong then the pendulum will spin in the reverse way to its normal rotation. If the choice of stone is confirmed as correct then you need to consider whether the stone needs to be re-energised. In this case cleanse the stone and place it in the next appropriate moon. Put the stone to one side until you have completed this process.

Making a wrong choice

There can be disadvantages in having access to teachers like the Arimathean and Elijah. Their knowledge is vast and they divine the purpose and the history of a crystal by having it placed in the hands of their channel. Sometimes this can leave me feeling a little inadequate. Will I misuse a crystal or get the choice wrong for a particular client? Elijah addresses these concerns:

The different kinds of crystals all may appear to be very similar in the way that they look and sometimes in the way that they react to the requests made of them, especially if a healing crystal is purchased in ignorance as a protective crystal and constantly used in that manner.

There are two main structures of crystal, and each has a different molecular structure which gradually alters if a crystal is used incorrectly.

There are crystals which are used for specific illnesses by healers who purchase them for a particular purpose. If they are chosen intuitively and if there has been very little preparation by those who sold them, then you may find that the structure is viable. They will adapt, especially if you are using your powers of programming correctly. So there is no need to fear that if a crystal is used for the wrong purpose that there will be no positive benefit.

Consider how many people purchase a crystal simply because of its beauty or because they have been told to buy a blue, green or pink crystal. They use it for their own benefit, when travelling, or place them around the chairs of people who are ill with no explanation given, possibly because none is known. It would be heinous to feel that all that healing effort placed into those crystals is of no avail.

Obviously if the correct crystal is used in the correct way, if it is programmed specifically for a particular purpose and if its structure is recognised, then the healing is much more powerful. Personally I would rather that no crystals were used at all than for them to be used for the wrong purpose, without the knowledge that goes with the correct vibrational rate for the illness or for the person who is ill.

In a later teaching, Elijah explains in more detail what happens within the inner structure of the crystal when being asked to carry out a task for which it is either not entirely suited or prepared:

We spoke earlier of the changes within the molecular structure if they are used in the wrong way. Imagine a crystal is put to one side, possibly in a dark place and not used. Then it is brought forth, placed on a shelf in a shop where people come, are attracted to it and purchase. You have two people: one such as yourself, who has a reasonable knowledge, the other just seeking a piece of crystal because we might have asked them to do so.

Intuitively you would be looking at the crystal for a particular purpose; the other person would be looking for a colour, because we said 'green, yellow or blue'. They are not in the least anxious whether they get one from a particular country, whether it is clear, cloudy, multi-faceted or whatever. They take that crystal home content within their mind that it is for self-healing.

Usually we have followed through and explained how to programme their crystal and they do this, and yet, very possibly, that crystal was intended to bring a positive vibration of energy for other things, possibly to help energise other crystals, or to be amongst plants.

Some crystals should not really be used for human beings, they have been in the earth a long while, they love the earth, they love that which grows from the earth. Take a piece of crystal that does very little for you and place it round the roots of a plant that has not flowered for a long while and watch it flower. So you need many different kinds of crystals.

But this new seeker after the truth of crystals does not know this and is quite successful in using that piece of crystal for his or her own use. But if you tried that, it would be a disaster because already you know so much about crystals, about their energy, their structure and how to use them. Your own thoughts move into the crystal, programming it from that very first moment. So therefore the structure within it begins to alter, move and flow from the time you purchase it. When you bring it home and programme it for the purpose that you want, it will either succeed or not, because of your own knowledge. Not a very comforting thought, we realise this, but nevertheless your thoughts, your knowledge have a great influence on what you will receive from the crystals that you buy.

We know that sometimes you will buy a lot of small crystals in a box without choosing individually. You can sell or give those crystals to anyone and they can do what they like with them, they will be quite happy. But you take one piece and you decide because it is clear it is for essential healing and you programme it for bone structure. It will revolt because within itself it knows that it is perfect to cure nerve pain and not to heal bones.

Preparing crystal elixirs

Q: Are there specific types of crystals which can be placed in spring water, made into crystal elixirs, and then drunk on a daily basis to strengthen crystal healing treatments, or to maintain general good health?

A: Most of the polished crystals can be used in this way, amethyst, tiger's eye, name whichever you like, any of those that have been polished for hand holding (not malachite, which contains copper), *because they are small they are ideal to place into water reservoirs. More particularly we prefer the amethyst because this does work on an inner level of the organs, the kidneys, liver and the intestinal tract. The tiger's eye can be used if there is a problem with the gall bladder or stones virtually anywhere within the body. But, of course, you can also use the polished amethyst as that will pulverise the stones as the water that has been around it passes through the kidneys. So rather than confuse people we would say use the amethyst for this and keep your tiger's eye in order to protect your home by placing it on window sills.*

Creating harmony in a meeting room
Q: Can you recommend a stone which is useful for this purpose?

A: We prefer that one particular kind of stone is used for general protection such as that of the home. If you use a large protective crystal to bring harmony to the many energies from different people in a meeting place, then that large crystal should be placed away from other smaller crystals. It should be from a variety that truly understands its purpose and which can remain energised all the time people are within the room because if it begins to lose its energy that can be detrimental to the harmony of the people who are all together

I use smoky quartz and an elestial for this purpose. In the directory of crystals the teachers discuss a rose quartz which has other minerals within it, and say that that particular combination has a protective influence. They have also mentioned tiger's eye and rutilated quartz as protective stones. There is more than one variety of stone to choose from, but in my experience the common denominator is smokiness, or density.

Trusting your intuition
Do use your intuitive powers as much as possible. If an inner feeling is that you should not use a particular crystal or indeed on an occasion just use your hands or channel the Christos through, do listen to your Higher Self and do interpret it in the way that you feel is correct.

Some of you are aware of different forms of healing and again your intuition should come into play. As you have been following the instruction that has been given to you through ourselves, you may find that some of it conflicts with your tuition through other sources, particularly the written word. It is entirely for yourselves to decide in what way you translate the information that you receive from different sources. Where it is possible to balance the information equally, to make your choices so that you are able to help your patients adequately, then it is to the good of all concerned.

Testing the energy level within stones
If you are using a stone frequently, or on the first occasion of using a new

stone, do use your pendulum to test its strength. Rosalind counts down steadily from 100% while the pendulum circles over her stones and assesses precisely the level at which the stone is operating each time she uses them. I tend to check my main stones every now and again with a pendulum, but often it is through the touch, sight or an inner message that I become aware that a stone I have been using is 'tired' and, just like a person, 'needs a break'. Then I cleanse it, often leaving it in some natural well water for some days, and wrap it in silk or velvet. I check it from time to time, with my pendulum, to see if it is rested before placing it in the new or full moon depending on its nature. This routine might go on for a period of time until I sense that the energy in the stone is restored.

Caring for crystals
Crystals are living organisms which will continue to change and grow within your possession. They absorb the energies around them and redirect them into the atmosphere and energy field surrounding the people who use them or keep them within their home. As the Arimathean once said:

People who have a perception of crystals will see quite a lot. If a crystal is neglected, almost permanently, never spoken to, never cleansed, it becomes dried-up, ugly, but as soon as you begin to show a little care, it is like a baby, it begins to blossom and to open up.

Crystals magnify and amplify energy. During a healing that magnification and amplification is part of the conscious process, the energies evoked harness the Earth energy and its connection with the God force towards healing. However, crystals will continue to work wherever they are placed in your home or work area, whether you are consciously aware of this or not. Therefore, it is important that all your stones are well maintained and frequently cleansed, in order that the vibrations which they emit are positive and directed towards the purpose that you have dedicated them for.

Why some crystals break from use
We asked Elijah a question about why crystals sometimes break for no apparent reason. His explanation answers not only this point but provides some insight into the internal structure of the crystal:

E: Sometimes crystals break so easily and you ask yourself, 'Why on earth has this broken? It was hardly touched, or it fell such a short distance'. The reason is that it is physically over-tired and stressed and needing rest.
   Like the human body when stressed, every particle within it tenses and becomes rigid. It is like an icicle in a cave. As soon as it is touched, a tip breaks off and the beauty of that drop of water becomes distorted. The energy needed in order

to remain frozen in that way is colossal. You cannot begin to understand the stress that takes place. Of course within crystals this is compounded because crystals have a centre, they have a heart structure, not unlike the heart structure within nature. All that takes place within an area is reflected and absorbed by the crystals.

I am fortunate enough to be able to X-ray stones for you, to see exactly what is occurring, whether that crystal is working to its full power, or whether there has been an imbalance within it at some stage of its growth or in its journey, or even in the way that it is being used.

The pure clear crystals specifically for healing are very tough, very strong but once they begin to have energy movements (which appear as shadowy traces or frosting within a crystal) *they should be treated very gently as it is possible, without any mishandling, for different parts of the crystal to crack and to break.*

The molecular structure of a crystal such as this (Madagascan clear quartz with three distinct bands of frosting inside it) *is extremely varied. Therefore, as the energies move toward the surface there is a break or a rupture deep within its centre already beginning. After a while, depending how often the crystal is used, the movement appears on the surface and the crystal may break in several places. A crystal such as this should not be subjected to the sun under any circumstances.*

To illustrate the point, he speaks of the reactions of the crystals which surround him while he is talking:

As we speak with you, we are aware of a lot of responses all around us. Our words are appreciated in a different manner by different qualities of life. Human beings understand the words, the vibration of the speech that we give. Animals go by the intonation, the rise and fall of our voice and the familiarity of certain words. But within inanimate, but highly responsive life such as crystals, every particle vibrates to the sound of our voice, as they are familiar with our energy because of our role in relation to them.

Removing 'old' memories from crystals
The Arimathean gave the advice that cleansing the crystal in the way described below, before use, and placing it in the appropriate moon is sufficient preparation before using a new working crystal. If you should feel that in a particular case the cleansing has not worked, because the crystal does not feel responsive, then you could try this:

Put it in a dark place. A crystal sleeps if it is in a box or if you wrap it in silk and put it to one side somewhere, or just cover it in velvet cloth and leave it. Then it will sleep and you would have to programme it again when you bring it back into the light and wish to use it.

Q: How much time should I give it?

A: A week should be sufficient.

Whichever method(s) you choose, do use your intuition, or your pendulum, and confirm that the cleansing process is complete and that old memories have been fully removed.

Cleansing
Do cleanse your crystals before using them for yourself. This is in order to remove the vibrations from their last owner or from the experience of being mined, hurled about, covered in dust and stored away from natural light.

The method the Teachers advise is to soak each crystal separately for 24 hours in sea salt water and then to examine it to see if you think it is thoroughly cleansed. A further soaking in clear water will cleanse away any salt residue.

I tend to put my crystals that work together, do the same task, or are stored together in the same bowl. I place clear quartz in separate bowls according to their purpose: healing; protecting; meditation etc. All of the calcites which I use for healing go in together and I separate all the lighter stones (above the waist) from the dark (grounding stones). Tourmaline or obsidian, (stones that absorb) are always placed in individual containers. Stones which are used for specific conditions are always kept apart, and I cleanse wands and pendulums separately.

If the stone is too fragile or large to be submerged in salt water then holding it under running water is acceptable. But water, either running or still, is the Teachers *only* recommended method of cleansing.

Rosalind wished to find a way to remove the 'crust' which settles on some crystals and asked the Arimathean what natural method she could use, rather than resort to acid which many dealers use:

A mixture of vinegar and water, possibly the white vinegar which is a little less harsh. The kind of vinegar you would use with your meal, not fruit vinegar as such. It is, I suppose you might say, the sour wine, which is actually sold as vinegar.

Q: Do you leave it without taking it out, just until it comes clean? Do you need to keep changing the water?

A: Overnight; should be sufficient depending on how much you have diluted it. Another method you can use, but it is harsher, is to put it into diluted bleach.

Cleansing obsidian
Obsidian is excellent for absorbing radiation from computers and televisions but, if used for this purpose, then do cleanse it on a regular basis. Place the obsidian in a glass of salt water on a window sill separate from your other stones. Once you have used an obsidian to absorb radiation then it needs to be

kept separate from your other stones as it can transfer, and amplify, the radiation into them. The long-term absorption of radiation by other crystals will damage them. But the regular cleansing of the obsidian will enable it to continue to absorb radiation without causing damage either to the stone or to you.

How do I know if a stone is cleansed?
Does it shine? Is the surface clear and free from any tackiness? If in doubt, ask your pendulum. Consider 24 hours as a minimum, keep the crystal either in well or salt water, freshened each day, until you feel it is ready. Once you are satisfied that it is cleansed, the next step is to energise it in the moon.

Energising
Put your crystal on a window ledge, or outside if the weather is frost free, for 24 hours before and after the new or full moon. The new moon is more gentle and the clear crystals prefer that gentle energy. Opaque crystals and the more robust and deeper colours benefit more from the full moon.

Elijah once shared his surprise that putting stones in both moons can cause them some difficulties:

We have been told by some people that energising done during the full moon can be reversed if the same crystals are placed under the new moon. This surprised us greatly and so we have done a few experiments and have found in some cases this is indeed true. There is a particular family of crystals which have within their structure more than one specific energy field. These do not react well if they are placed in both aspects of the moon. The full moon is very energising; the new moon has a much quieter effect upon them.

So experiment for yourself. Place different families of crystals outside in a frost-free environment for all the phases of the moon (full, new and quarter days) *and then test with your pendulum to see if they have changed. If that is the case then you will know that you should not energise that family of crystals during both phases of the moon. You will know to choose just one, and to keep the crystals out of direct moonlight during the alternate phase.*

We have found generally that with the humble plain quartz you can do anything and it will be quite happy to oblige, but if you use crystals such as the denser rose quartz, the aquamarine, in fact all the greeny-blue crystals, these should only be activated at the time of the full moon. The very soft crystals, those that crumble easily and break when they are knocked, need the gentler, quieter energy of the new moon. Put them on a window sill overnight, not outside or in the rays of the sun. So you see we also learn by trial and error in order that these expensive luxuries are neither broken, nor yet work outside of their intended purpose.

Using equipment to energise stones
We understand that there are units that have been especially prepared, scientifi-

cally, in order to energise crystals and some people use laser crystals. (Elijah is referring to the laser crystal, usually a point between 4 and 6 inches in length which tapers naturally to a point, rather like a finger.) *We feel it is not necessary to use them. They are artefacts and usually the energising is comparatively short, suitable perhaps for the client of that moment. After a while it can indeed impede the energy field of the crystal itself. We do not encourage people who work with our methods to use artificial artefacts if natural processes are available. It is very quick to use a laser to charge other crystals, especially when people are doing a lot of healing, one person after another throughout the day, and they have one laser that they use in order to energise many different stones, then it is a quick way like a battery charger. It gets the healer out of an awkward situation.*

If you take a little longer over your preparation, then it should not be necessary to use the artefacts, except very, very occasionally. All you need to do is to keep your different stones energised and stored in natural conditions. You can, if you wish, have more than one set of a particular stone dedicated to healing and alternate between sets to allow time for cleansing and re-energising between clients.

Natural light (not direct sunlight) *is of course perfect for all crystals, but in some cases natural light is not available so we have no objection to artificial light.*

Programming and dedicating

Some people use the term 'programming' and some 'dedicating' when informing the crystals about the purpose that you wish them to serve. Before I go into detail about how to do it, you might be interested in this response from the Arimathean about the difference between the two:

You can dedicate the crystal, with your own free will, toward a particular purpose because you feel a relationship with it, you feel it is suggesting to you that that use would be excellent, or that a particular use should not be considered. Therefore, because of the energy which is being radiated between the crystal and human there can be a dedication to the crystal to say, 'We understand your inner awareness, your inner need; we will use you for that purpose as long as you desire it. If you desire to have a greater or lesser purpose in our relationship together, we will be aware of this as long as you are as strong in your ability to convey this to us as possible, then we will be just as aware as we are of your need now.'

Now there are, of course, many people who would say, 'What absolute nonsense', but those are the people who shouldn't really be using crystals anyway, because they don't have a particular rapport with them, they don't understand the basic teaching regarding the humanity of crystals.

But the programming is where somebody might take a crystal and analyse it rather more structurally, with the brain rather than with the heart. They would say, 'My brain says that you are good and strong and sturdy, you will withstand knocks. I feel good with you, I feel you are protecting me. I am going to set you up to do just that.'

So there are the two ways of approaching crystals and what you are going to use them for. Both are all right but briefly: dedication is from the heart; programming is from the mind. Both are perfectly acceptable.

How to programme or dedicate a crystal

Whichever approach you choose, your crystal needs to be informed about the purpose which you wish to use it for. Think of a short affirmation, for example:

> 'I want you to work with me in meditation, to inspire,
> guide and protect me.'

If the crystal is small enough, place it to your third eye and repeat that affirmation several times in your mind, directing your thought towards the crystal. If the crystal is too large, hold a smaller piece of cleansed crystal to your third eye and repeat the affirmation. Then, point it at the larger crystal and direct the thought pattern from the smaller crystal into the larger.

Storing

Where possible store crystals in natural light (but not in direct sunlight) or in artificial light if necessary. If the opaque crystals are placed on purple cloth and the clear crystals placed on gold, the vibration of those colours will assist them to replenish their energy. I would suggest keeping your crystals on, or wrapped in, silk or velvet, especially if you carry them around with you. Fragile stones will break if not well protected during transportation. Be careful of the splinters – they can be very sharp.

Do be aware that crystals love light. If you keep crystals wrapped up and deprived of light they will eventually fall asleep and need to be reawakened when you wish to use them. Some years ago, before my partner had the benefit of Elijah's advice, he did a healing using a crystal wand which was owned by his patient. It had been wrapped tightly in silk for several years, it was so starved of light that when he put it to use it absorbed all the energy that was meant for the person, thereby negating the positive impact of the healing.

Enhancing their impact

If crystals are lit, say on a light box, (a stand on which a crystal is placed, with a gentle light source which illuminates the crystal, usually from below) or placed under running water, the gentle warmth of the light bulb or the movement of the water releases the crystalline particles into the atmosphere. Water and warmth have the same effect as holding and stroking a crystal. Using a light box gently warms a crystal, and placing it within running water accelerates the amount of energy that is released. Either way the effect is to increase the amount of energy released into the atmosphere, which can then be absorbed by those people who are close by.

We created a crystal fountain and the atmosphere changed immediately when the water first tumbled over the loosely gathered pieces of rose quartz we had placed in and around the water spout. Later we bought a piece of rose quartz drilled specifically for that purpose and the impact lessened considerably. The Arimathean later explained that the trauma of being drilled takes its toll on the energy within a stone, like people they become traumatised. So try to avoid drilling or cutting the stones with metal implements if you wish to get the maximum impact from fountains or specific displays. Try to use the pieces which, although they have been through the mining process, tend to recover more quickly if they have not been drilled as well.

Where to keep them

The crystal should be placed where it will be used, for example keep your meditation and self-healing crystals where you usually meditate.

I would advise against keeping a selection of crystals in a bedroom, although clear quartz crystals can assist to replenish your energy field, and stimulate self-healing while you sleep. If you wish to do this place two clear Brazilian quartz crystals, which are regularly cleansed and energised in the new moon, one on the window sill behind your curtains or blinds and one on the top of a cupboard or shelf near where you sleep. Here they will pick up the energy from the moon and circulate it within your bedroom.

Mixing crystals together

The energy field of crystals interact one with another. Their energy pattern reflects their country of origin and the place from which they were mined.

As a general rule, try to store crystals with space around them and, if possible, by country of origin. This avoids the different vibrations clashing and creating a sense of disharmony which some people are very sensitive to. I tend to store crystals from the same family, and of the same colour together. I keep the light quartz together in a group, the dark quartz in another and the calcite in a third group etc.

The size of the crystal is a guide to the amount of space which you should leave around them. You can, as an experiment, allow your pendulum to start spinning over a crystal and then move slowly away from the crystal until the pendulum stops rotating. This is an indication of the size of the energy field of that particular crystal. As Elijah once said:

Powerful crystals can produce flaws in others. Large and powerful crystals should never be placed in close proximity to smaller crystals, as indeed flaws, very serious flaws, can develop. Have any of you ever found that, when some of your smaller crystals are in proximity to larger powerful ones, that they have broken or have lost part of themselves? You may have suddenly noticed that a chip, or a crack, has appeared, and wondered to yourself how this occurred.

Once you have arranged your crystals in a display, be aware that introducing new crystals means introducing new energies. I keep new stones completely separate from any crystals that I use for healing, until they have been cleansed, energised and dedicated. I store my working stones in separate wooden and felt drawers, and add any new healing crystals either to an existing group of the same type, or to a separate compartment. I add silk to keep individual crystals apart from one another.

Even with display crystals I tend to keep the new crystals apart for a while, until I have a feel for where they should go and which of my other display crystals they will mix well with.

Storing according to the colours of the chakras
If you are storing a collection of tumblestones in a vertical display then do arrange them, as much as possible, in alignment with the colours of the chakras, the light above and the darker, heavier ones below. This does make a difference to those who approach your display as their energy field interacts with the different energies of the stones. Imagine facing a shelf of black tourmaline which is level with your third eye!

Chapter 6

Basic ground rules

It is best to have principles and adhere to them, and not to allow clients
or friends to feel that you are hesitant over these principles.

The Arimathean

Crystals are very powerful and often their power does not become apparent until you have started to work with them, maybe experimenting with a grid. Here are some basic ground rules which it is recommended that you follow until your connection with the crystals and the spirit world is so well established that you can afford to trust your inner guidance completely.

Even then, speaking personally, there are some rules here that I would not break. They include the first two about pacemakers, working with people following certain invasive treatments, and working with pregnant women.

Pacemaker alert
The presence of crystals can affect the functioning of a pacemaker. This is true if the environment contains active crystals as well as if the person presents themselves for healing. Therefore the advice is not to offer crystal healing, and to ask potential clients or students if they have a pacemaker fitted before inviting them into a healing room laden with crystals. (You can put crystals to 'sleep' by laying silk or velvet, the darker the better, over them and giving a clear mental instruction for them to sleep. See page 143.)

Chemotherapy or radiotherapy
Crystals can adversely affect people in receipt of chemotherapy or radiotherapy. This is because they are likely to increase the sensitivity of the body which in turn may affect the rate at which the chemicals, or the radiation, are absorbed by them. Therefore, it is advisable not to offer crystal healing to people in receipt of chemotherapy or radiotherapy, or during the six months following completion of their treatment. The specific advice from the Arimathean is included on page 85.

In respect of laser treatment, it is recommended that you do not offer crystal healing until three months after their treatment has been completed. This allows their body to heal, recover and regain its strength and to be in a better position to accept and utilise the energy of the crystals.

The placement of crystals – some golden rules
Q: Are there any golden rules, for example using heavy, opaque or dark stones only below the waist? Is it always sensible to use stones in a layout that echo the colours of the chakras?

A: That is very important. There have to be a few basic rules that a new student can easily remember and adhere to. Imagine an outline of the body including the meridian and chakra systems with all their colours. Across the centre of the body, between the solar plexus and the heart chakras, place a dividing line so that all the darker colours appear beneath that line. Across that dividing line, below the vibrant heart chakra with its merging greens and bluey greens, imagine a thick emerald green which is merging down towards the lower trunk and upwards towards the ribs and the heart. This emerald green is the balancing colour which allows all aspects of the body to harmonise together.

When I do a layout either side of the chakras I usually use one type of crystal – quartz, for example – or perhaps two different varieties from the same group. For example, I might place five citrines above the waist, and two carnelians, one at the knees and one at the feet to ground the client. As a rule I apply the advice presented above in the following way: I use the lighter stones, such as clear quartz, along the entire length of the body, but confine heavier and darker stones to below the waist.

You will notice that in the basic healing grid on page 101 there are two green calcites, placed like guy ropes either side of, and just below, the solar plexus. The placement of these stones is designed to promote emotional stability during the healing.

Advice for pregnant women
Q: I have always been cautious about working with pregnant women. If I relate back to your description of the chakras and the meridians, we do, of course, have an entire baby below the waist during pregnancy. What advice would you give?

A: As a child's chakras are forming and the meridians are in a very delicate stage of being created, the adjustment one to another is not there until shortly before the birth so interference in the growth pattern of the child could take place. In general we feel that crystal healing is not really suitable for pregnant mothers. Having said this, on one or two occasions it can be beneficial, but you need to know the mother well and know that they are sensible in their approach to healing and use (cleansed) *crystals already as part of a self-healing routine.*

So generally it is much better to say that once somebody knows they are pregnant, do not do crystal healing on them. Do spiritual healing. They shouldn't be denied healing, of course not, but spiritual healing is really the only form of treatment that is totally safe.

Q: How far does this extend? For example, if pregnant women have crystals within their home?

A: If they have a protective crystal in their room or in their vehicle, or wherever it is needed; if they have a crystal for its beauty, for its calming influence; if they have one that they display when they are relaxing to music or listening to poetry or anything else that is a relaxant for the body and for the mind, they can be encouraged to use that as much as is necessary.

But the active crystals, used on the body or in relation to the body, should not be used. They can do their self-healing technique with an affirmation and prayer, but not with a crystal.

Q: In the case of pregnant women, would it be true to say that collections of stones have more potential to exert a negative influence than single stones? A bowl of tumblestones, for example?

A: Indeed, it is better to put them out of the proximity of the mother. So cleanse them, cover them, allow them to sleep in a darkened place and then after the child has been born cleanse them again, awaken them in the moon and put them on display once more.

Healing children

The Arimathean gave some advice to the parents of a young Child of Light addressing their concern that the baby had been negatively affected by a health worker. I have included his response because it covers work with all children who are, in his words:

... self balancing, especially a Child of Light. As long as they are loved and any physical problem eliminated, such as flatulence or anything of that nature, because a child can be very uncomfortable if they have any of those problems.

If you are concerned that some negative influence has upset the child:

... then simply hold the child, reaffirm the love, the energy towards it, and place the hands around the body so that the healing energy flows very gently from mother, father or healer to the child. The essence is gentleness and softness, nothing 'taken out', nothing 'put in' and in general we would ask that you do not attempt to heal a child under six months; take them to an expert.

Q: You have advised, I think, that crystals should not be used until a child is over two years old, but could you use a rose quartz with a fretful baby?

A: Certainly not at close proximity. It could be in the room, but preferably the other side of a curtain on the window sill. There are a lot of problems with attempting to heal the very young using crystals so we advise that you just gently touch their head using only your hands and bring the Christos energy through, that is all.

Q: If a child had diarrhoea, would there be any value in giving it some spring water in which amethyst had been soaked. To cleanse the system?

A: That is a little contentious. Very difficult with young babies. We would advise not. Before the age of two they have their own defence system, the immune system. It is very strong when they are born and should not to be interfered with by other practices. It is a natural immunity to certain things which might otherwise attack a young child and make its survival difficult. After the age of two it is usually possible to introduce gentle, delicate crystal healing to good advantage.

Stones to use with children over two years old
Rose quartz: Can help a young child to sleep. Place on a window sill behind the curtains or blind.
Amethyst: Can assist a child to be alert enough to gain energy from its food.

In both instances one of the small polished stones would be best. (But kept well away from an active toddler who might put them in his or her mouth.) *In illness, after seeing the practitioner, which is very important, these small gentle non-intrusive stones can be used in connection with gentle spiritual healing.*

Complying with official guidelines
The Arimathean and Elijah strongly recommend healers to advise people who want crystal healing to contact their doctors and to follow medical advice. They advise crystal healers to stay within the rules of the appropriate governing bodies within their country:

A: We would not go against what official bodies think is a wise procedure. (Within pregnancy) *there can be repercussions on the healer if anything goes wrong with the subsequent birth, or the child is born dead or malformed. It would be highly unlikely that the healing, whether with or without crystals, had caused it, but in order to save the healer from distress, we accept it is better not to treat the prospective mother, nor yet a very young child with crystals,* **unless there is a specific written request and a statement from the guardian that they accept all responsibility for what might occur.** *In that case healing can then take place, but no healer should ever request the discontinuance of any medication given by the official sources in the medical profession, because that immediately could trigger action against them, not only against the individual practitioner, but possibly against the parent organisation to which they are attached.*

Q: Would you say 'no' to spiritual healing if somebody is pregnant?

A: Personally no, we would not, but with the same proviso that they should sign a little paper, pre-prepared, that they accept total responsibility for the healing taking place. Then the healer would record the kind of healing and the duration of it on that form at the completion of the session.

Q: The parent organisations do provide pro formas for people to follow and parents are asked to give consent before any healing takes place on their child. Part of this process is to ensure that the parents have sought medical advice.

A: *We understand it is the same with animals regarding veterinary attention.*

Q: That is correct and we need permission and assurances that veterinary advice has been sought and followed.

Compilers note: The Affiliation of Crystal Healing Organisations (ACHO) provide a Code of Conduct and Guidance to Practitioners. This document includes pro formas for written permission before working with children and animals. It lists a number of standards to which crystal healers, qualified through programmes accredited by this organisation, are held accountable.

Respecting the medical profession
Both Teachers have always held the view that the future for crystal healing lies in working cooperatively with allopathic medicine:

A: *It is so very important that the healing professions do not seek to undermine or take over from the medical profession in any way at all. It has never been proved to the satisfaction of the British Medical Association (BMA) that healing in any respect either improves or heals totally any condition that they might seek to help. All the while this takes place those within the complementary healing professions must be suitably aware of their responsibility.*

Chapter 7

Preparing to heal

I know the God within.

The Arimathean

Often people start by offering healing to friends and relatives and it is easy to focus more on your need to practice your new skills than on the needs of your 'patient'. However, the impact and the power is just the same. Once someone has experienced crystal healing the pattern of energy that was created will remain within their aura and the spiritual connection will have been established, whether or not they experience anything tangible at the time.

When I have been given advice about running training sessions, I have been told not to take anyone without knowing their full medical history (see page 84) and not to undertake practice sessions on someone unless they need that particular healing pattern.

You can create grids without having a 'client' in the middle of them and still experience their energy field. Whatever you do, use prepared, dedicated and energised stones which you keep for healing. In a workshop setting, people should use their own healing kit and take responsibility for it before, after and during the session.

Healing for the first time

This handbook does not pretend to provide an exhaustive list, but regardless of whether it is a friend or a 'client' you might like to consider the following practicalities well before the appointed time:

What you need to do to create the right ambiance for a healing session, especially if the room has multiple uses.

How you can be assured of privacy and quiet during the session.

How you would summon help, if needed, and indeed let the client know that someone else is on hand.

Whether you will ask a fee for the healing session or whether there is to be a mutual exchange of energy in some other way.

What steps you need to take to prepare yourself, the crystals and the room beforehand.

The range of (prepared) crystals that you need to make available. See the basic healing kit, see page 86.

You will also need to consider where to store your crystals so that they are easily accessible to you during the healing, but outside of the energy field of the client (6 feet or 2 m away) until needed. This is to prevent all your crystals mingling with the aura of your client prior to them being selected and placed in a grid. After you have made your selection you should ensure that only your selected crystals come within that 6 feet (2 m) area.

On a very practical note you will need a table, or flat area, within reach where you can place your working crystals. You are likely to be laying out at least twelve stones at the beginning (five in the protective grid and seven either side of the chakras) and collecting up seven at the end of the session, plus you will be using your wand, and perhaps your pendulum. Because your client is very quiet and still, and needs to feel safe, it is important not to walk around more than is necessary and not to clatter the stones together if at all possible.

Taking a personal and medical history

When I first started healing I went through a standard set of questions, and it took a while for me to ask myself what I was looking for in the answers. 'What would I do if ...' – type questions kept arising for me, and I realised that I needed more clarification before some new client was sitting in front of me, looking expectant, while I tried to organise my thoughts and find the courage to say 'I am sorry but ...'. So, here are my questions and all the advice that I received on what to look out for in the replies:

Q: I ask for contact details and their age. I have not been asking for their date of birth. Should I?

A: The date of birth will often be quite important when you come to analyse the reasons behind the illness. The sign under which they have been born is often an indication of the kind of illness that will occur during their years of life. You need to be aware of their age, the multiples of seven, so that you have an idea that when the whole body, all the cells, change each seventh year some of them might produce an illness. So we feel that it is very important for you to know the actual year and date of birth.

Q: I ask them why they have come to see me and what they hope the healing session will address. I ask the following questions in relation to their medical history:

Whether they:

have ever had any epileptic fits – petit mal or grand mal
have ever been treated for depression
could be pregnant
have a pacemaker fitted
are in current contact with their doctor
are taking any medication
have been in receipt of chemotherapy or radiotherapy

I ask about:
their parents and the illnesses which have been, or are, present
within their family background

their current use of complementary therapies
their emotional and home situation

I give them the chance to add anything that they think I should know.

A: Very comprehensive. Now, to what extent do you feel it is lacking?

Q: I don't know if anything is lacking. The question for me is: if a 36-year-old client who has come to me because they have stress in their life tells me they had an epileptic fit when they were young, does this mean I cannot treat them?

A: Not if it was as long ago as that, because fits are quite prevalent in the early years of life, especially if the children are Rhesus negative, which they may, or may not, be aware of. Fits can also begin at the time of puberty. But it is not the occasional fit in childhood that is the main concern, but whether they are registered as epileptic and whether it is petit mal, which is occasional and does not require medication. If it is grand mal with medication, that could be interfered with by crystal healing. With any form of consistent epilepsy, we suggest healing without crystals and no stirring up of the sensitive areas within the brain with regression.

Q: What about working with people who have been receiving chemotherapy or radiotherapy?

A: We would not advise it. The potency of a natural product such as a crystal against the active ingredients of chemotherapy could be rather drastic. It would possibly accelerate the amount of chemotherapy in the body, which would be very drastic indeed, and therefore we would not recommend that this takes place. So you could add that to your list of questions. We would also add that within six months of completion of a course of chemotherapy or radiotherapy the use of crystals should not be encouraged.

Q: If they ask to come and have some spiritual healing, should I allow them in the sanctuary where I keep my crystals?

A: No.

Q: Is that because the healing room itself is a potent room regardless of whether healing is taking place there?

A: It is indeed.

Q: When we have spoken in the past, you have advised against using crystals for people with clinical depression, and in fact the necessity of keeping them away from potent environments where crystals might stir up problems for them. I would particularly avoid working with people taking psychotropic drugs. Do you agree?

A: Yes, and in these cases simply say that your healing centre is organised for crystal healing and therefore is not suitable to give them healing in any other form. If they wish to seek spiritual healing through a practitioner who does not make use of crystals in any way within their sanctuary, then you suggest they do so. This way it is up to them to be aware and to ask that practitioner any details they feel are necessary. It is their responsibility.

The basic healing kit
As stated earlier, one of the joys of the particular approach taken by the Arimathean and in particular by Elijah is that healing should be simple and inexpensive to provide, especially for people who consider themselves to be 'beginners'. Speaking as a healer who relies entirely upon layouts from this source I can affirm how powerful they are when compared to many of the healing layouts suggested by other healers.

In order to explore and experiment with this method further, I would recommend that you collect a basic healing kit. In this way you can use cleansed, dedicated and energised crystals, which are used to working with each other, to explore the different layouts, combinations and crystal shapes. It may be disappointing to you not to have pages and pages dedicated to the magnificent variety of crystals and stones that are available and to concentrate on half a dozen only, but as Elijah says:

You have actually asked that a book be prepared for people who know virtually nothing about crystals. How can we launch into all the complications of these hun-

dreds and thousands of available crystals to those who perhaps only wish to use half a dozen, when we know that that half a dozen can bring about exactly the same results as hundreds of other more complicated, very expensive crystals? As far as I myself am concerned, I find that that which is simple and effective, reasonable in the outlay and cost is far better than a magnificent display which would possibly mean that the clients concerned might have to pay more than they can really afford. With this softer, simpler way everyone can benefit. It is the way of Elijah to try and encompass all rather than a few.

Where energy is concerned, energy is free. It comes from a central source, it pours into mankind, it is God-given, but we also realise that those that harness it and use it must also live. But it is not necessary from our point of view that all the beauty which surrounds people needs be harnessed at the same time. Do stay with the simple methods, they are much more effective.

Q: When you talk about having six healing stones, I wondered if there are six stones that every healer should have in their kit bag. Are there six key stones?

E: *We would say that the important stones which should be used would all be of the quartz crystal in varying sizes, and that the crystals should be as clear as possible. That would be a standard kit, whether it is two, three or more; the basic healing stone is quartz. No one will find that their condition degenerates through it. However, were you to use, say, a turquoise in the wrong context you could accelerate the illness in some way.*

What follows is the information that he or the Arimathean have given during their various teachings, plus my personal experiences.

Clear quartz
The major universal stone because it aligns so closely with the chemical make-up of the human body and the pure vibration rate can be easily accepted by so many people without any adjustment. It is at its most powerful when it has as little movement (cloudiness) *within it as possible.*

My experience: I use clear quartz to energise and to harmonise. It might well be the first stone I use to see how a new client reacts to crystals. It is certainly the stone I use to provide a strong protective grid around most clients and to stimulate and harmonise with the other crystals and energies which I am using. The Arimathean suggests clear, double-terminated Brazilian quartz for self-healing. Recently the Arimathean reminded me that clear quartz should be the first choice when working to improve mental impairment.

It is within my clear quartz collection that I have found my stones for specific uses including mending fractures and providing inspiration on nutrition.

Rose quartz

A universal stone because it is of the quartz family and therefore the statements above apply equally. In addition it is very calming, especially for people who are feeling agitated or anxious about visiting you. When people are very severely mentally ill, if they were to carry a small piece of rose quartz it would be the equivalent of many of the harsher drugs which are prescribed for them. So you could carry a small piece and if you are with someone who is unduly agitated, ask them to hold it for a little while.

The Arimathean gave a lovely teaching to Rosalind one day which explained the creation of a piece of rose quartz that she had brought to him. It is of such general interest that I include it here:

There are those pieces that are not clear, that have a cloudiness, a mistiness, that has been drawn from the rock but which has not developed out of the crystallisation of the water. There are two processes:

When a rose quartz is developing within a cave, there is first this crystallisation which grows over the millions of years which cannot be transparent. It must be opaque. It has mixed within it other mineral elements which come down with the water from within the cave, or from the hillside, or even as a result of the infiltration of sea or lake water. There is a solid rock base beneath the crystal which stabilises it and gives it a true purpose.

Then there is that which falls from the roof of the cave as the water becomes condensed. The water rises and because of the thin atmosphere it adheres to the cave and it drops, drops, drops on to a rocky base and it is very clear. Very often the cave is extremely cold, and the droplets freeze as they come down on to the rocky surface and they remain frozen long enough for its clearness, its clarity, to settle. As the process of condensation continues the clarity remains and builds up.

So, often you get a mixture. When man comes, he disturbs this and takes large formations of this rock which are almost clear. Very often there is very little of the deep pink colour produced by the minerals, it is almost like clear quartz. When it is formed and placed within the shop there can be confusion as to whether it contains several elements or only one. We feel that this piece has within it a mixture of different elements including zinc, but only enough to form it, to give it structure and balance. That which is clear and beautiful on the surface is that which was formed through the process of condensation and that makes it very clear.

My experience: I use rose quartz very widely for its subtle and diffuse energies. It produces the mental calmness described above and also evokes a receptivity within the body. This enables the healing energies to gently surround and enfold the client and initiate the self-healing response, often leaving a lasting sense of calmness and attunement. The Arimathean has suggested that other therapists use rose quartz near or under the couch, to calm agitated clients, to provide a vibration of love and sympathy and to soothe children. My partner, a psychotherapist, has a large piece of rose quartz in his consulting room which helps to create a safe atmosphere for his clients.

Amethyst

A member of the quartz family. Has a dual effect of calming and of exhilaration. It can bring calmness to those that are overexcited or anxious. When that subsides, it can allow more of an exhilaration to take place, so that people can appreciate the environment, enjoy what is happening around them.

My experience: I use amethyst as a cleansing stone. It is often one of the first ones which I use with new clients because it has the 'safety' and the universality of quartz alongside the more energetic vibration which can help to dispel the toxins from the body. I feel that the sense of exhilaration mentioned by Elijah evokes the self-healing mechanism quite strongly within the client and makes a good introduction to the healing process. Amethyst, when heated, turns white and then yellow and becomes citrine.

Amethyst can be drunk as an elixir: a small tumblestone duly cleansed and dedicated, within a jug of spring or purified water can have a cleansing effect. A glass of amethyst water each day can help to cleanse the body and can be beneficial in stimulating the kidneys, or removing calcification. But if the effect is too strong and diarrhoea starts, then cease the treatment.

Rosalind has used points of amethyst in the same way and found that the glass jugs broke because of the energy directed through the pointed shape. She would advise using tumblestones at all times. She also uses an amethyst cave (madonna) to energise crystals prior to using them for healing. You can place crystals on a bed (druze) or flat piece of amethyst to cleanse them.

Citrine

Is recommended by the Arimathean for clarity and decision-making and also: *In general we use the yellow citrine, or the golden, as many call it, for problems within the upper respiratory system. We also use rutile for this particular condition. If people have a growth within the lungs or bronchial problems, or even if the throat is inflamed, then we find that the yellow citrine and the rutile are excellent to enable the breathing to become more easy.* Ametrine is when a mixture of amethyst and citrine appear together.

Smoky quartz

Smoky quartz is often mentioned by the Teachers as having healing potential. The Arimathean has suggested to a Craniosacral therapist that a smoky quartz could be used to assist with a hyperactive autistic child, and a smoky quartz with rutile could be used to calm people who are emotional. In these cases the stones should be placed under the massage bed, towards the solar plexus area.

Again all the considerations of clear quartz apply, although I find the dusky stones more absorbing than the very clear stones. When it has a yellow hue it has a calming quality. However, note the reply the Arimathean gave when asked if they cook some of the smoky quartz in order to make it darker?

A: We suppose you could call it a form of cooking, certainly it is heated a great deal to allow it to darken; in fact heating is quite a common practice to enhance the energy fields in many crystals, but of course in doing this the natural energy field is virtually destroyed. We would suggest that when very exotic crystals are purchased, and by exotic we mean those clear ones with absolutely wonderful patterns within them, that the seller is asked most carefully what processes those crystals have undergone before they are sold. If there is still movement within the crystal, if there are still lights, and rainbows, if these are still apparent and change is taking place, then all is well. But if they are simply full of light with no moving energy then the whole process has been overdone, a realisation which always causes us pain, especially as they can cost a great deal of money.

Q: But if you take one that's been cooked or made darker and you put it beside another one that hasn't, can it receive the energy from the other crystal or will it take without giving?

A: It takes without giving.

My experience: A clear, gentle smoky stone can be very powerful and has a strength which is calming within it. Often, with the natural smoky crystals you cannot see the yellow hue, or smokiness, within one until you compare it with another, the colour is so subtle. I have a yellow standing point, which is almost the yellow of citrine and when lit it shines like a candle flame. It is one of the purest healing crystals within my collection.

Green citrine
This is a stone which the Teachers mention time and time again, but to date my searches have not found one. If you have such a stone in your collection then you might be interested to hear that it has the following properties: *There is a beautiful citrine which is moulded and which falls into its shape when it is fractured from the whole; it is akin to a square but between a square and a triangle. Usually they are fairly large and very heavy. The green is a very delicate pale green which usually is only apparent when it is placed next to another colour. It is a perfect healing stone to equalise energies within the body, especially within the blood. It has the same structure as quartz and is very good for heart conditions, for the regeneration of the brain cells following a stroke and reduces the active lipids within the blood stream which cause congestion of the aorta.*

Calcite

Elijah refers to calcite as 'one of the favourite healing stones'. The Arimathean describes calcite as having the following healing qualities: absorbing, softening and calming. Green calcite, for example, is very calming, honey calcite is more grounding and blue works with the mind.

My experience: A good universal stone with a variety of colours, making it very versatile. The colours include: green, gold, blue, honey and red. It has a soft gentle energy not unlike rose quartz but with a subtle power due, I think, to the different vibrations of the colours within it. I will often work up towards calcite in a series of healings, starting with any other quartz listed above and then introducing calcite, the more translucent the piece the better. I always use the lighter colours towards the top of the body and darker ones below the solar plexus. For example I would use the honey calcite below the solar plexus, often at the knees and feet. Calcite has an opacity and a depth to it which belies its strength. Do not let the fact that it is gentle distract you from its power.

The types of stones

In order to start healing you will need three types, or shapes, of crystal: some sets of tumblestones, a good wand and three double terminated crystals.

Tumblestones in any of the above varieties will be useful. Calcite is difficult to find in tumbled form so small pieces of rough calcite will do just as well. Sets of seven of each will enable you to create chakra layouts.

Crystal wands are shaped and usually have one rounded end and one pointed. I think a clear quartz wand is the most versatile. A smoky quartz wand is absorbing, very good for cleansing the aura. An amethyst wand is cleansing and energising. In most, but not all, the energy goes through the wand towards the point. When you first purchase a wand use your pendulum to check the direction of the energy flow.

Their main use in crystal healing is to direct, and harmonise, different energies and, when used on their side, to cleanse the aura. You use a wand within a healing grid to join up all the stones and to open the heart chakra to signal the start of the healing. Rosalind asked the Arimathean about wands:

They do give a very specific energy force which is direct or is directed toward the purpose that is being created for the healing. We would never suggest using a wand as part of a grid beneath a couch or a chair because of the energy which is created by electric impulse, or at least by the electrical circuit, within the healer which is directed in their mind towards a particular purpose. A wand responds very greatly to the mind of those who use it.

For example we would not recommend that a wand is handed around to other healers. If there were two healers working in a room with their clients and one of these healers did not have a wand with them, we would not recommend that the other healer lends theirs because a wand is very closely aligned to the owner.

Q: Generally speaking should healers always use their own crystals and not lend them to others?

A: *Yes, but particularly so with a wand.*

Q: Is there another purpose for wands?

A: *You can use a wand to unite different crystals which are not yet part of the working programme. For example if you are going to use four or five different crystals and place them around or beneath a client, then you can use the wand to unite their energies.*

A wand laid in the centre of a circle of crystals will often create a ring of energy around those crystals, harmonising them. But you have to be very specific in your use of these crystals. For example, if you placed them around a larger crystal or around a candle, you could evoke a pattern of circular energy but it would be very difficult to do in advance of your client arriving.

Once crystals are all united by the energy of a wand, if you want to separate them and use them for different purposes, you would have to disengage that energy force. (by closing down the crystals, as you would close the chakras, see page 105).

Double-terminated crystals (DTs) have a point at each end. They do form naturally, or can be carved, but they need at least one unbroken termination at each end. Personally I use three natural DTs in all, two of which are similar in size, either side of the heart, and one at the feet. The one I place at the feet is substantially bigger as it assists with the grounding process.

Those are the main healing stones which the Teachers advise us to use in the basic healing grids. They have energising and general healing abilities, and are the least likely to cause adverse reactions in clients who may be very sensitive to crystal energies.

The main grounding stone within this collection is the honey calcite. Therefore, you may feel that you would like to add a specific grounding stone, for example tourmaline, see page 126, for those situations when you find it difficult to ground a client at the end of a session. Once you have completed the grounding procedure outlined on page 106, if the person is still feeling a little light headed, you could place any one of the grounding stones listed in the directory between their feet, while they sit and talk with you, about the healing session and their reaction to it.

The directory of crystals on page 125, lists the other stones for which the Teachers have given specific guidance, and includes their advice both healing, and for other uses, such as to improve environments.

The basic healing techniques

The main reason why crystals should not be placed on the body is because of the fluctuation of the aura around the body.

The Arimathean

In order to start the healing process it is important that you are comfortable working with a pendulum. The reasoning behind this has been covered on page 58, and is addressed by Elijah on page 145. I think that it is important to work with your pendulum to reinforce your own intuition, and to build confidence in yourself and your own connection with the crystals. With this, as with so much else, I do not advise that you give your power away to the pendulum, but maintain your own level of discrimination and evaluation.

One of the ways in which you might use your 'people pendulum' is to assist you to ascertain those areas which may need a little extra attention. To find out if the pendulum is of assistance, try this exercise a few times on a partner, to practice your technique and to build confidence.

Using your pendulum with a partner

At this stage in the book I will stop reminding you that all stones that you use should be cleansed, energised and programmed for what you intend to use them for. Remember if your pendulum goes in a direct line then it is showing you that it is not ready to work at this time, or it has not been adequately programmed, or you are not asking your question clearly enough.

This technique can be useful for checking out the health of a client before they come to see you, or even if they are with you, but is particularly useful for distant healing:

Exercise 6

> **Pendulum exercise**
>
> Select a person to work with.
>
> Move to separate rooms having agreed that your 'partner' will concentrate on their own health and sensations within their body. The exercise lasts about fifteen minutes, so do ensure your 'client' is comfortable and able to rest undisturbed for that time period.
>
> Establish a mental link with them.
>
> Spend five minutes exploring that mental link. See what images you get of their energy field, of sensations within their body, of health or emotional difficulties. Take a couple of minutes to record your thoughts.

After five minutes pick up your 'people' pendulum and see if using it makes your visualisation of their energy field or body any different, clearer or more easily defined. Make notes. Continue for five minutes and then take a couple of minutes to record your thoughts.

If you are taking it in turns with a friend, then change places at this point, prior to discussion, so that the second person is not influenced by the responses that the first received.

Take it in turns to discuss the information that you both received and how accurate you each were with or without the pendulum.

The questions to consider are whether the pendulum:

increased your accuracy?

increased your confidence?

provided you with a useful tool?

Starting a healing session
There is no 'one right way' of healing and so I am sharing my normal practice with you as an illustration rather than as prescriptive blueprint. Your practice, and mine, will change to meet the evolving needs of clients, and to reflect our own development as crystal healers.

Before setting up any of the following techniques you will have set up your healing environment, taken the client history, and chosen and prepared a range of crystals to select from.

Selecting crystals for use with clients
While I am talking with the clients I am also assessing the crystals that I should use. Sometimes the choice is based on their condition; for example 'I have cancer' would indicate celestite as my first consideration. More often it is to do with the type of energy they are describing: 'I want to be calmer' would lead me to consider rose quartz; 'I need more energy', clear quartz. Sometimes, the name of a crystal, or the sparkle of a crystal on a shelf catches my attention and I will always check that out. For example, in one session a crystal I had never used before suddenly came to mind. I used my pendulum to confirm the choice (see page 60). Sometimes, however, the pendulum disagrees and then I would not use that particular crystal.

Once I have chosen the type of stone, or stones, then my next question is which chakra should I place them next to? If the colour and density of the stone dictates that they should be used above, or below, the waist then that would take precedence. But if I have a choice of two stones both of which could be used along the full length of the body – for example, clear quartz – then I might ask the pendulum which stone should be used on each chakra.

If the pendulum confirms citrine on the crown and third eye and clear quartz for the remaining chakras, then I check out whether the stones can work in harmony, and if the chakra set will work with the protective grid, or any other stones that I may have chosen.

Placing stones on the body

I am about to describe two healing grids, which are essentially layouts of crystals designed to create a positive energy field in which your client lies, or sits. It is important to note that these grids do not include placing stones on the body of your client. Occasionally clients might hold crystals, but I never place them on their body because of the following advice that the Arimathean gave:

A: The main reason why crystals should not be placed on the body is because of the fluctuation of the aura around the body. We would almost use the word 'the fibrillation' of the chakras and different energy centres. They are not stagnant, they are not flat within the body with no life of their own, they have a lot of life of their own. They are like little star bursts that every now and then move out of the body structure into the auric body. This is very important for the body itself to maintain its rhythm, to allow the changes of energy to take place and keep the healthiness and balance of all of the body.

You know yourself that if you are sitting very close to somebody with whom you have no rapport, you keep edging away, hoping they will not move closer, and you feel that any touch or closeness from them is literally an irritant to your body and stimulates its protective system. The protective system of the body does not like anyone, or anything, coming in very close, unless it has become attuned.

If people wear crystals on their person, on chains or anything of that nature, it becomes personalised to the wearer. If there is an energy within that crystal that is not acceptable you will very quickly find that people stop wearing it.

So imagine a whole series of different crystals being placed on a body, some of which might have been used for different people and not adequately cleansed – this does happen – or which are not attuned to that person's body. What happens is the patient begins to move, to squirm a little, to try to throw off the crystal that is aggravating them. They are not relaxed or absorbing the healing. Therefore, it is better if the crystals are laid away from the body where they can radiate towards it, then the defence system of the body can come into play if there is anything that it really cannot accept. This way the whole of the crystal layout can do the work it is intended to do, without creating any pockets of irritation.

Generally speaking you are not committing a crime if you put the stones on the body, but some of the chakras are more sensitive than others, especially the solar plexus and the forehead. If you put some of the stones on the forehead even the chill of the stone can create a feeling of repulsion. If you put something that is an intense energy, which could really help to maintain the well being of the person, onto the solar plexus, that might evoke a severe jolt in the protective layer. So it is far better that this is not done.

Q: As you speak, it occurs to me that the natural reaction of the body is to instantly close down its protective system. Therefore if you evoke this protective response in a healing session it is counter productive. The idea is to work gently and slowly so that the body is open and able to receive healing?

A: Yes, it is like a foreign energy coming in and creating a negative reaction, which means, perhaps, that the relaxation and absorption doesn't take place until the last few minutes of the healing, which defeats all its purpose. So we do adhere to this. If you explain why in the book, then people will appreciate this and any patients will know that they will be able to relax. Who can truly relax knowing that they need to lie immobile, and that any movement, or twitching, will shift the whole lot off the bed and onto the floor?

Q: I had stones laid on all my chakras at a time when I had a cough. Every time I coughed they all fell off and had to be replaced. I found myself choking to try and stay still.

A: Very probably the cough was accelerated because there were some crystals there that your body just did not want to accept.

Q: Is it relevant that, if you place the crystals about twelve inches (30 cm) from the body, you are placing them in the emotional aura? Is that by design, so that the emotions can accept the healing and then move it into the physical?

A: The health aura is very close to the body itself; we would say about two or three inches (5 – 7 cm), and therefore, yes, the emotional aura would be between eight to twelve inches (20 – 30 cm) away from the body. Individual auras do vary, but those are the sorts of distances involved.

It is important that the emotions can accept what is taking place in the healing, then the health aura can take on all the responsibility of the absorption. The emotional body takes time to absorb what is happening in the health aura, which is why sometimes an illness has taken root before the personality realises it, and then it takes a longer time to shift it from the health aura and the body itself. If, during a healing, the emotions are rather mixed, if they are saying: 'Well, this is all right but I am not feeling anything', it is because the emotional body needs time to dwell on it and to work out for the self the principle of the healing.

The exception to the rule
As with everything as soon as you say 'never' you find that there are exceptions

to the rule, and in discussion with Elijah he explained that you can hold a crystal on the body if you are bleeding somewhere:

Let us talk of that for a moment or two. Surface bleeding, which has been caused by a cut or a knock, can be helped by placing a crystal on the wound. If you suffer a burn from scalding water or touching something hot then you can put a clear quartz crystal straight on the place for as long as it needs. It cools and it heals, and it is safe to apply crystals in this way.

    Do you ever place your crystals to the third eye and feel whether they have a warm or a cool energy? Do you know that for healing burns you want crystals that feel cool, but if you are working with something like a cancer you would want them to feel warm? The grey area is arthritis or osteo arthritis; for these conditions the stones should have a 'cool' energy but for rheumatoid arthritis you would use 'warm' crystals.

Undertaking a healing session

In this section I am trying not only to describe a healing grid, but a healing session. When I was training, often I found myself trying to imagine what a healing session might look like as a whole, rather than just a selection of techniques – so here is how I do it. Elijah provided a healing grid, for people who are lying down, and it is this one that I use most frequently.

Having chosen the crystals and placed them more than 3 feet (1 m) from the massage table, (this is to prevent all the energies merging with the client's energy field until I place them within the grid) I ask the client whether they would like music during the healing and make a selection which suits them.

The client removes their shoes and lies on a massage table. When working with crystals, a massage table which has a wooden construction allows more energy to reach the client than one which has a metal frame. (Once I had a client for whom removing their shoes was a difficult procedure. The Arimathean assured me that the healing energies would pass through her trainers quite adequately.)

I cover them with a silk and velvet cover to keep them warm and check whether they would like a pillow beneath their knees. If they have back problems a pillow under their knees does prevent them putting pressure on their back.

Lying down is not always essential; for example, some children

Protective grid

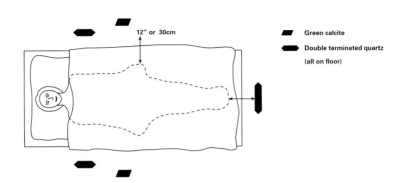

12" or 30cm

Green calcite

Double terminated quartz

(all on floor)

would rather sit. If clients have heart problems, remaining seated assists the circulation, although the legs may need to be slightly raised. A reclining position is ideal. On page 103 I provide a grid for working with a seated client.

I have the ability to further extend the width of my bed once the client is settled. This allows me to lay out the stones that I have chosen to work with the chakras about 12 inches (30 cm) from their body, but level with it. If this is not possible for you, then place the stones on the floor around the bed. Or, if necessary, settle your client on a mat on the floor, but maintain the twelve inches (30 cm) distance between the stones and their body.

I ask that they close their eyes and then I quietly earth myself and relax to enable the connection to be made. The affirmation that I use is 'I know the God within'. I invite my guides and teachers to work with me, and for my client's teachers or guides to be present. I ask that I may retain the light that I need to maintain my own well being.

Rosalind begins by earthing herself, and then standing at the head of the bed, placing her hands on the shoulders of her client and sounding three Aums, (see page 13) either silently or with them if they are familiar with the routine. She adds the word 'Shekinah' after each Aum (see page 15) and visualises a spiral of crystal energy, filled with the light of the Christos, entering the room, to provide protection, and to fill the space with light, colour and healing energy.

As the client relaxes, I talk them through a visualisation, which often begins with them relaxing and concentrating on their breathing. I suggest when they breathe out, they visualise anxiety or negative energy leaving, and as they breathe in, this is replaced by a golden light, usually emanating from a star or similar symbol. (see single cell principle on page 16.) I ask them to imagine this golden light gently entering through their crown chakra, and filling their body with a sense of wholeness. If I know they have teachers or guides that they relate to, I suggest that they invite them to be present.

As I talk them through the visualisation I put the protective grid in place (see page 99) by laying five stones on the floor, about 2 feet (60 cm) from the edge of the table. I place the two double-terminated clear quartz crystals either side of the heart chakra, in line with their body and a large double-terminated quartz at their feet, across ways. When placed, these three crystals form a circle (or spiral) of energy around the bed. From their solar plexus in a diagonal line, like guy ropes on a tent, I place two light green pieces of calcite, slightly outside the circle of the clear quartz.

Once the first crystals have been placed on the floor I always walk in the direction of the spiral, and avoid entering the energy field of my client near the crown chakra. I also try to minimise the number of circuits that I do.

I use a wand to join up the five stones by visualising a line of energy linking them. I do not touch the stones but point the wand at them, and pause over them as I walk round. I start with the stone to the left of the heart, draw in the guy rope from the solar plexus to the first green calcite, and then continue to the stone at the feet. I draw a line from the green calcite on the right to the solar plexus, and then move to the stone to the right of the heart. After the first circuit I only work with the clear quartz and the spiral, I do not keep re-drawing the line between the solar plexus and the calcite.

Once the spiral is in place (usually it takes two or three circuits), I place the seven stones chosen for the chakras, working in a

Basic grid

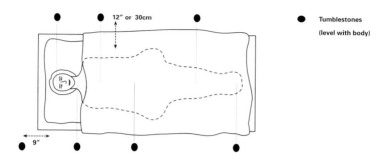

clockwise direction. I place the stone beside the crown chakra first, to the right of the crown, and then going down the left-hand side of the client place one stone to the left of the third eye, heart and knees and, moving up the right-hand side, beside the feet, solar plexus and throat. All the stones are placed at least 9 inches (22 cm) away from the body.

I take the same wand and join up the stones, starting with the crown chakra, crossing the body to the third eye (which passes over the third eye chakra) and then back again to join with the throat chakra and onwards down the body, creating a web of energy over the client. I create a line with the wand that joins the feet chakras to the double-terminated stone at the base of the bed; this is for earthing.

As I move back up the bed, to sit or stand at the crown of the head, I start the healing process by briefly touching the wand close to the heart chakra, without touching the body. In my mind I say a brief affirmation, 'Let X receive the healing that they need at this time'.

Sometimes I take another crystal to hold while I sit at the crown, usually a rounded enhydro (a quartz with water within it) or simply use my palm chakras to direct the crystal energy through the chakra system. You could, if you wish, move out of the energy field as the crystals can do the entire healing for you. However, I tend to remain within the energy field and to add a little directional healing through the crown. I feel I can monitor

Practice guideline 5

the healing more effectively by remaining within the energy field, and am more alert to changes in the client.

Rosalind sometimes uses a green serpentine, when she is working at the crown. I mention this here because this crystal is very gentle and balancing. She uses it for a client with heart problems which it is particularly suited for, but in general it is good to consider this stone for anxiety and stress or where a client might need more balance.

I tend to use crystals at the crown which do not have a termination. I hold them in the palm of my right hand to enhance the healing energy which I am directing through my palm chakras. I am looking for a diffuse, rather than a directed, energy as that might be too invasive at the crown. I hold my hands about 9 inches (22 cm) from the top of my client's head, and although I usually remain seated for the entire time that the crystals are working, I would not undertake healing through the crown for more than twenty minutes at a time, usually closer to ten.

A grid for a seated client

Sometimes the client, or you, decide that remaining seated would be the most favourable way of working. I often suggest that children remain seated for their first session.

A basic grid is to place one grounding stone under the chair and two double-terminated clear quartz crystals, one in front and one behind the client. Put these DTs, about 3 feet (1 m) from the chair, length ways so that they create a circle or spiral around the client. Place two pieces of green calcite either side to the front of them just outside of the clear quartz circle, so that they can act as guy ropes from the solar plexus. Activate the grounding stone first by using a stirring motion with the wand, raising the energy towards the chair, and then draw the guy ropes in place with the wand. Walk clockwise, as in the first grid, to join up the spiral.

If the client has a specific condition, they can hold the appropriate stone in their left hand. Often clients bring a favourite crystal with them. If it does not conflict with the grid, I usually let them hold it during the healing. If I have a query, I will dowse the stone with my pendulum to ensure that it will not cause any problem when mixed with the other stones.

Once the grid is in place, you can stand behind the client and work through the crown chakra in the way described above. You would close the session in the same way as if they were lying down.

Seated grid

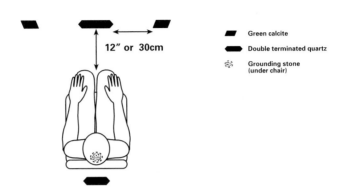

12" or 30cm

■ Green calcite

⬡ Double terminated quartz

⊛ Grounding stone
(under chair)

What happens during a healing session?

What happens during a healing session is very individual, both for the healer and for the different clients. Fundamentally, I would say that I wait, watch and protect the sacred space that has been created. I used to feel I ought to be doing things, like checking for heat or coldness in some areas, but I don't need to do that so much now, partly because I have reached a point where my etheric self is working with me. However, as you can see from my question to the Arimathean, I had to overcome my own disbelief.

Q: When I am working, I seem to be able to affect healing by thinking about the parts of the body or the parts of the aura that I wish to affect without having to move. Is that in any way real? Can I, or any healer, just stand back and use thought projection?

A: That is because the crystals and yourself have become receptive to one another. You have concentrated so greatly on harmony, on doing the best you can for your clients. You put yourself out of the picture and allow your etheric self to move with your crystals to make the best possible response to the person on your couch. In theory all healers can do this, in actuality very few do.

You are inclined to think about your client after the session, plan the next one, hope that he or she will continue the healings until there is an appreciable difference, even a complete healing. A lot of healers do not do this; they switch off completely and after the client goes they barely remember their name, let alone their condition. So that person will be less likely to have the link either with the crystals or with the harmonies of the body of their patient.

Q: I have not been sure whether to trust my experience, and yet it seems a much more sensitive way of working because there is less disturbance in the room. It seems more subtle and responsive because the degree of concentration is so great.

A: Of course, the patient can relax and not feel that their aura is being invaded or touched. The lack of words, of a verbal response, is always good. Gentle music in the background – something that soothes both patient and healer – can be an advantage. But the human voice has tones within it that can at times be very harsh, very sharp but then again on other occasions so understated, so delicate, that people can barely grasp the words that are spoken. That can be just as irritating.

Aura brushing

One of the techniques, which can also be used for self-healing is to use the side of a wand to 'brush' or 'cleanse' the aura. This can be done at any stage during a healing session, and may need to be repeated. I compare this with skimming the scum off the top of stock – not a pleasant analogy but an accurate one. As the crystals start to work, the energy field of the client moves and reacts and heavier energies are disturbed. By taking the flat side of a wand, pointing it away from you, you can brush these energies out of the aura and into the earth.

You sweep in a single movement, about 2 feet (60 cm) above the body, from the crown chakra over the body, past the feet and on to the floor beyond your earthing crystal. I usually sweep down towards the feet once over the midline and then once again down each side of the body. My standard practice is to aura brush, after taking the chakra set away and before I close the healing session. This ensures that any negative energies are swept away. But throughout the healing I check whether it is needed at an earlier stage, for example if I sense a lot of energy rising to the surface and then settling.

Rosalind sometimes uses this procedure prior to starting the healing itself and then, at a minimum, three times during the healing. She sweeps the wand down the left side of the body, up the right hand side and then down over the chakras. She visualises the etheric counterpart (see page 104) of the wand working on the other side of the body at the same time.

Judging the length of the healing session

You will develop your own sense of when the session is completed. I experience a mixture of sensations. Often the energy field from the crystals is so strong that moving my body is difficult and that is a clear signal that they are still working. Sometimes I feel an imperative to: 'Stay with it ... stay with it ...' or 'The healing is complete, but give the client time to recover'. As a rule of thumb the average time, once the crystals have been activated, is 20 minutes, but this can be significantly less with children, especially Children of Light, and can extend if a client has had a number of sessions.

I have had the experience of one client reacting very strongly to the crystals being laid around their body: their body jerked in a way similar to an epileptic fit, but without the violence of movement. My first instinct was to quickly remove the crystals but I was guided, quite firmly, to 'stay with it', which I did. In retrospect I realised that an early and rushed response would have caused more problems than staying with it and allowing the body to relax and achieve the emotional release that was so badly needed in this case.

The safety and the comfort of the client is paramount and in a different situation it may be necessary to slowly remove some of the crystals closest to the client in a planned way and replace them with gentler and more soothing crystals to relax the body. In my view it is working with confidence and with calmness that is so important.

Closing the healing session

When I consider that the crystals have completed their task and any aura brushing has been completed, I very quietly collect the crystals that have formed the set beside the chakras and place them outside of the energy field of the client. Usually I aura brush at this point, but only if I feel it to be necessary before closing the chakras.

I do not pick up the crystals which have been placed in the protective grid on the floor, or under the bed. To dismantle all the grids with the client still in situ can, for some sensitive clients, prove a little disturbing. It is better to let them leave the energy field themselves.

Closing the chakras

I always close the chakras because they have been stimulated. I use the method advocated by the Arimathean:

We would suggest that you use your crystal wand and start at the feet of the client in order to prevent anything from moving through the entire body and into the chakras at the soles of the feet.

Hold the wand flat, pointing away from you and circulate it over the chakras in the soles of the feet and the knees. Then holding it flat, with the point away from you, bring the wand up the body in a sweeping manner until you get to the solar plexus. Circulate the wand over the solar plexus, continue up to the heart chakra, the throat chakra and then the crown.

What you will find is that the wand will pick up the different energy flow from the chakras and will tend to want to go either clockwise or anticlockwise, alternating as it goes. As you close each chakra circulate the wand in line with this pattern. I usually find that I close the chakras in the feet; solar plexus; throat and crown in a clockwise direction, and the knees; heart and third eye in an anticlockwise direction.

Once I have closed the chakras I normally make one last sweep with the wand about 9 inches (22 cm) above the body, starting at the central line, and then either side. My final closure follows the advice from the Arimathean:

After you have made the closure with the wand, say a little prayer or something suitable for the closing of the session, giving thanks to those spiritual helpers around both of you for their assistance, their comfort and their protection

Grounding the client

Because crystal healing increases the vibration rate of the client's body, and often increases their mental and psychic awareness, they do need your assistance in bringing them 'back to Earth'. To do this I concentrate on their feet and the ankles, in order to bring the energy, and their consciousness, down towards to their feet.

Once I have closed the chakras, I place my wand outside their energy field and then walk to the end of the bed, hold their feet and ankles, and very gently ask them to bring their consciousness back to the room and to imagine the golden light surrounding them and being encased within their aura.

One visualisation that I use is to ask them to imagine that the gold light that surrounds their aura is similar to the feathers on the wings of a bird. They can close that golden light around them at will, protecting the light and colour that surrounds them. I remind them that the light comes from an inexhaustible supply, and that by connecting to the earth through the chakras in their feet they can transmute any heavy or negative energies, and draw in the golden light to replenish them, and to bring a sense of well being. As I speak, I gently touch their feet and ankles and touch the chakras in the soles of their feet.

Rosalind has a more detailed routine: she holds the soles of the feet and then takes the ankles and pulls gently three times. She massages the sole of each foot three times in a clockwise direction, left foot first. She pulls gently on the ankles and holds the soles of the feet. When moving between the two feet, she is careful to keep one hand on the body at all times to prevent the energy of the massage being broken.

At the end of the grounding procedure I ask them to open their eyes in their own time and stand back from the bed to give them some space. The Arimathean advises:

Move away from the client and allow them to come round properly and get up from the couch. If, of course, they are in any way distressed you must then give them a little more healing. Seat them, rather than lie them down again, and just go around their body with your hands evoking golden energy so that they are protected around their aura.

Pouring out a glass of water at this time can be very grounding. So I pour out some water and hand it to them to drink when they are ready to sit up on the bed.

I guide them off the bed, away from the protective crystals that are still lying on the floor and back to their seat. I leave the crystals in place and remove them after they have left the room.

I find that some people feel the cold after receiving healing energy and so I am ready to offer them some form of warm cover while they are recovering.

Having grounded your client, do not forget your own need for grounding. The crystals do not just affect the client, they raise your vibration rate and sensitivity too.

Some clients do need a while to ground themselves following a healing. This can vary between clients but also between sessions depending on how powerful the session has been. When booking the appointment you might want to mention this to your clients, especially if they are planning a long drive or preparing to return immediately to a business meeting.

Chapter 9

Keeping records

After my clients have left, I pick up all the stones and leave them under running water. I cleanse them in the same groups as I have used them, the chakra stones, the protective stones etc. Rosalind puts hers into sea-salt water for at least one hour. I make brief notes of each visit using the following headings:

Session number, date and time.

Feedback since last session – at the start of each healing, except the first one, I spend some time discussing their feedback from the previous session including:

Any changes since the last healing?
Any reactions or responses in the few days after the last visit?
Any change in their condition or any of their therapies or medications?

After the session I record:

The stones and the layouts that I used.
Patient feedback.

My assessment of the session – a short self-reflection on the healing. What I have learnt and how I will apply it in future.

Any adverse reactions?

This routine of keeping notes started when I was studying and from time to time I would think, 'Oh it's only X or Y – partner, son, neighbour – this is not a *real* healing. I don't need to keep notes.' But it is these very people who came back six months or a year later and I found myself wondering what I did the first time. It has also been useful to look back over my progress and to see how quickly I have advanced and modified my techniques. Under the ACHO guidelines it is a requirement that I keep accurate notes, which enable me to be able to answer any queries from clients but also to encourage me to reflect on my own practice. Remember that these notes and the medical history that you took before the session contain some very personal information and therefore need to be kept confidential and safe.

Once you have completed the paperwork, do allow yourself a short time to restore your energies before either the next client or the next task. If you have a self-healing crystal, this would be a good time to use it.

Beyond the basics

Generally speaking, the most wonderful purpose of any healing
is to enable the cessation of pain at any level.

The Arimathean

In my experience working on the whole of the body is very effective and I have not felt a pressing need to start refining the technique to cover specific areas of the body or conditions. Crystal healing is essentially holistic and constitutional, but there might be times when either you wish to concentrate on one area, or may need to confine the energy of the crystals for some reason.

One way in which you can supplement the basic grid is to put additional crystals under the massage couch. If you do this, then you need to use a wand in a stirring motion to get the energy to rise to the level of your client. However, as Elijah has recently cautioned, placing a stone directly under a tumour can be over-stimulating and might actually progress the illness. There-fore, he suggests placing it on the floor, at least 2 feet (60 cm) away from the body, and to one side of the tumour. If a tumour is present, it will be activated along with the rest of the body, so you need to decrease the impact of the surge in energy by placing it slightly to one side of the affected part, or below the waist and in the centre of the back in the case of breast cancer.

Here are two grids for specific areas of the body and some advice on how you can extrapolate from these two examples the general principle behind grids.

A grid for eye conditions

Place four aquamarine stones on the floor, two either side of the head, level with the eyes, and two either side of the throat, forming a square. Place one double-terminated clear quartz on the floor at the feet of the client to allow the energies to circulate. Place no other stones on the floor with this grid.

To join up the four aquamarine stones on the floor, take a crystal wand and join up the two level with the eyes by moving the wand between the two stones seven times, as you would when joining up the protective grid in the basic grid, then join the throat stones in the same way. Move clockwise around the bed pointing the wand at the clear quartz to get the energies to circulate.

Take a small wand, dedicated only for this task, and circulate this in a clockwise motion three times around the outside eye socket, about 6 inches (15 cm) from the body. Keep the wand moving. (See Elijah's advice on working on the eyes in Appendix 1, page 140)

Proceed by sitting or standing at the crown chakra and using your hands to direct energies rather than additional crystals.

Grid for eye problems

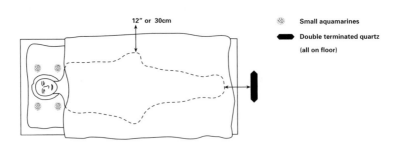

A grid for kidney problems

A grid for kidney problems

On the floor place an amethyst under the head, an aventurine under the lungs and a red jasper under the bladder. You can place a protective grid of clear quartz around the bed first and use the wand to activate the crystals under the bed using the stirring motion described earlier.

Grid for kidney problems

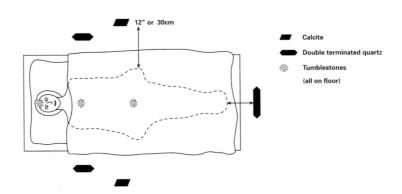

Cancer

When working with cancer or any condition where there is swelling, the Teachers have suggested that we use celestite under the bed to one side of the affected part, or below the waist and in the centre of the back when dealing with breast cancer. Celestite can be used in a combination with the protective grid of clear quartz, providing the stones have been dowsed to ensure that they can all work together.

Another grid for a cancer patient which I received during a meditation, and which I checked with the Arimathean, was to use obsidian alongside the client at their feet and knees, to draw through the negative energies, and gold and blue calcite above the waist to replace those darker energies with light. I have used a combination of this grid with the celestite underneath when someone was emotionally drained from the medical procedures associated with their cancer and their fear and their anxiety needed treatment almost as much as any tumour.

Creating new grids for specific conditions

In order to extrapolate from the examples that I have given, I asked the Arimathean if there was a general principle about the formation of grids that I could share:

Unfortunately grids and healings in general don't conform to such a nice, easy pattern. We wish they did, it would be simpler for many people.

Q: I am aware that the grid that you gave for the eyes is contained within the parameters of a square around the eyes. The grid for the kidneys is stretched along the whole body, and I realise that the impact of the kidneys, and the urine passing through the body, does affect the whole body. So is this a principle that can be applied elsewhere?

A: *Yes, the heart, for example, affects every cell in the entire body, so if you are treating someone with severe congestion of the heart, heart failure, a fibrillation of the heart or angina, you still have to treat the entire body. You would place your grid from the crown to the feet. But you would vary the content, the actual crystals that are used, according to the degree of pain or defect that you have within the heart. It would be a different grid for example for angina than it would be for congestive heart failure.*

Q: A different grid, or different crystals?

A: *Different crystals within the same grid, to be precise. What would you do if somebody came with loss of memory, someone who was very strong physically, healthy and without a particular weakness in any area, but who had received a* *blow to the head which has given them amnesia? Or if their loss of memory is due to a particular group of cells in the frontal lobe which are being destroyed by a virus or by cancer? What would you do in that case? What grid would you provide, bearing in mind this is not for the body, as such?*

Q: My first thought is to put citrine beside the chakra points and maybe an obsidian under the bed, under the head.

A: Why the obsidian?

Q: Just for mental alertness really.

A: Golden or snowflake?

Q: I would probably use rainbow obsidian and citrine, depending on the person, either down the whole body, or with some darker stones below the solar plexus. Is that anywhere close?

A: It's very close. But when you consider the importance of the brain to the reflexes of the entire body and how different areas of the brain work with the autonomic system or the person's awareness of the past, or of the present, there could then be quite a variance in healing techniques, different forms of crystals and minerals, and in some cases you might feel that a grid isn't really applicable at all. So it is in this kind of area that the new healer might need more understanding and more explanation than, say, if they were dealing with a defective kidney, sclerosis of the liver, or even a sprained shoulder.

As a general hint, always get people to look at the body holistically, and what is happening to the whole body when one area is severely affected. If it is a pulled muscle, it would be very different from a broken bone, or from cancer in the muscles or in the bone. If you work on that principle, you could end up with forty or fifty different groups of crystals and as many grids.

I know what we would do: we would take two clear quartz crystals and place them in the palms of the hands of the sufferer, place another crystal a little way away from the crown chakra, and then link the different areas of the body with a criss-cross motion with your wand. A wand is unique inasmuch as it has this wonderful blending. It is like moving energies from one place to another and linking them, which only a wand can really do; but otherwise we would have a very, very simple composition which incorporates the whole body. There could be another one, or two, reasonably clear quartz crystals at the feet.

Q: So creating a circuit, across and down and out.

A: Yes, because nobody is ever completely sure which area of the body is losing the synchronicity of the brain. Damage in one area of the brain can have various dif-

ferent effects, and of course we do believe in simplicity, that is very important, so when in doubt (you can say to your readers) rely upon the simple, clear crystal. You can never go wrong with it.

A timely reminder for me about losing touch with the core of the teachings and getting too complicated.

Levels of healing

The healing process takes place on a number of levels – physical, mental, emotional and soul. It may be that a client presents you with a physical symptom or set of symptoms and, after the healing session, the sensations that they report are primarily physical: 'tingling,' 'heat,' 'pressure' etc. Alternatively they may present emotional or mental difficulties and experience a greater 'peace' or 'understanding' as a result of the healing. It is more unusual, although not impossible, for a client to request that you put them in touch with their soul and their spiritual path.

As part of my thesis to complete my diploma, I evaluated each of the healings that I had done on each against the different levels but I could not think of a way to measure the impact of healing on a soul level. For the purpose of my own research I compiled evidence on the physical or mental or emotional levels combined. What follows is a meditation that I received from my own internal spirit guide while doing this work, which I have checked for accuracy with the Arimathean. I include it here because it provides a concise teaching on the different levels of healing.

'So you are seeing cycles in your research into your patients. Those who came with physical symptoms one week report mental improvement the next, and those that found mental well being on one visit report a physical lightness, a sense of well being.

'There is more than one reason for this. Firstly there is the way the crystals work on the subtle bodies where there is a built-in delay in experiencing the effect of the healing. Energy and colour absorbed by the emotional body take a while to be recognised and absorbed by the emotions themselves. There might be resistance within the personality, and the energy itself takes time to establish and to move through the subtle bodies into the awareness of the human being.

'The soul is playing its part. During the healing the soul is absorbing the light and the colour and, as you often see, it communes with aspects of its Higher Self during the healing, seeking guidance, upliftment and understanding. So the soul itself receives healing and participates in the level of absorption and level of acceptance. The soul, if you like, is the regulator. Time is needed for the soul to allow the energy to be imparted and understood. Without understanding and acceptance, the client will not realise that they have been affected on any level. That understanding and acceptance need time to establish and for the words to be found to share it with others and with their healer.

'It is the same on the physical level, the requirement for understanding and acceptance is as great as on the emotional level because the mind has to be engaged in the process of healing, of moving beyond the symptoms to the lessons and then beyond those into well being and vitality. Once again the impact of the healing takes time to be absorbed, for the person to recognise the lessons, their pathway and to choose to take it. This can sometimes take time because the realisation alone may not be enough to instigate action or change within the personality. That may take longer and require a drip, drip approach of consciousness, at a level and a pace that allows gentle absorption.

'The spirit world could provide the ultimate answer, the whole lesson, on the first request but usually it would be meaningless, and sometimes even destructive. Although some people desire blinding flashes of insight and "the road to Damascus" type of experience, most people usually benefit more from very slow and staged progression, regulated by their soul and their Higher Self. The slow, staged approach enables integration and the chance to make the changes their own, rather than accept some change imposed by a higher source that is in some way commanding them. This would be to deny their free will and would be contrary to Universal Law.

'So as you work you are looking at progressing through the levels, a spiral of progression moving gently forward, but moving through all the levels and achieving balance one by one. Sometimes you may find that the feedback is all physical, sometimes mental for a while, but the effect is holistic. It is just that one area needs greater concentration to achieve the initial balance so that you can then work steadily through each level.'

As a result of this work and understanding I usually ask clients to commit to three, possibly five sessions, in order to be able to work through all the different levels. The frequency between visits depends on the type of issue that they bring. If it is physical, I ask that they return weekly, if possible, for the first few sessions. If it is mental or emotional, I usually suggest a gap of about three weeks, this is because the healing moves more quickly into the physical body from the health aura, but more slowly when you are dealing with the emotional body and the response of the personality.

In my experience, the main exception to this is a Child of Light. The impact of the healing seems instantaneous and immediately recognised by all the different levels. There is so little resistance, it feels like holding a dried sponge in the sea and watching it open out and drink deeply.

When clients are undertaking a course of crystal healing with me, I advise them against starting new complementary therapies until the completion of our treatment sessions. This is to allow me to accurately monitor progress and to try to minimise any potential conflict between therapies. If they are in the middle of an established treatment programme I would not advise them to stop, but to advise the other practitioner that they have started crystal healing.

Managing your energy during healing

When I first started healing I felt very energised during the sessions but then quite tired afterwards. I asked the Arimathean whether it was possible that I was using my own energy rather than channelling energy.

You are probably relying very much on the energy of the crystals surrounding you to maintain energy levels within your body. Tiredness is quite natural; there is always depletion after any kind of treatment whether it is speaking with a client or using your healing ability. We would say the rush of energy that you feel is the energy coming down from the Earth and being utilised through your person toward them. You are not retaining it for long, you are allowing it to dissipate.

When the client has left, instead of the residue remaining within you, it has continued to be removed from your body and dissipating beyond where you can utilise it to much better effect. It is a mental process. As the energies come in and move toward your client, just say mentally to yourself: 'At this time I am retaining all that is needed for my own energy not to be exhausted, to retain the spiritual energy and growth within myself'.

Always make sure that between your clients you have sufficient rest, take your own self-healing crystal, and just have a quiet moment or two communing with it, allowing the termination to point toward your heart chakra. A few minutes should be enough to revitalise you, but sleep is also very good so we suggest that you have a rest whenever you can, just for 10 – 15 minutes.

Increasing your psychic awareness

I am sure I am no different from any other healer when I question the abilities that I have and feel that I will be a better healer 'if only ... '. I asked the Arimathean once what areas it would be useful for me to work on, and he replied:

Work on your third eye to try and perceive more surrounding your patients, so that you can be aware of conditions which are locked into their auric selves. You may not have the gift of perception through sight, but through your intuition or feelings. Whichever way you wish to develop you should concentrate on doing so.

You can start the process in meditation before they are due to arrive. Concentrate upon them and try to visualise their aura with the illness that they have mentioned when they made the appointment. See if you can visualise how it appears in the aura, say a malfunction of the kidney or the liver, how it affects the aura with the shadowing and the darkness of the area surrounding it. Sometimes, especially in the lower organs, it shows as a very dark red glow. With other areas of the body the red can be rather brighter, more scintillating, but any degree of red within the aura does show illness in that particular part.

When you look at your patient sitting in front of you, it might appear as a dark area within the misty whiteness of the shadow surrounding them. This gives you a visual concept of where there is trouble. If you close your eyes, you might be more intuitively aware of where in the body the pain or discomfort or illness lies.

When they are present, you can work with your pendulum to be sure in which area the illness lies, through the comprehension of your other senses, confirmed by the pendulum, Take your palm down and around the body, while holding your pendulum in the other hand, note any reversal in its swing which would indicate a problem in that area (the technique is described on page 45).

This is an holistic assessment, but where there are mental problems surrounding the patient, perhaps because they they have been in the company of people with negative energies, or working with them, you can perceive this through sight: the darkening of the aura, a lack of vibrancy, a lack of spontaneous light behind them when reflected against the wall.

We used to suggest at one time that healers sat their patients in front of a plain light wall, that they could then ascertain the aura visually with greater clarity. It is not so easily perceived against a patterned wall or one that is painted in a dark shade.

Detecting negative energies

Q: Can you advise me how to detect and deflect negative energies?

A: You can rely on your senses – you either feel drawn to a person or wish to hold them at arm's length, as it were, not wanting to be particularly close to them either physically or mentally. Those with dark intrusive forces will endeavour with their eyes to comprehend your own awareness, your own sensibilities. You might feel a reluctance to meet them eye to eye, or to allow yourself to be taken in by them. All these are little clues to help you foresee problems that might arise with those that visit you, or are asking for a crystal healing session. Always take these instinctive feelings very seriously, do not cast them aside as paranoia or over-sensitiveness.

Q: If I feel uncomfortable, should I then proceed with the treatment?

A: We feel that if they were truly negative there would have been a sufficient indication at the time of making the appointment to cause hesitancy. If you are just a little unsure, make sure that someone else is in the house and is alerted to your apprehension. You could perhaps have a bell that is situated within easy distance of your hand, so that you can ring if any real difficulty comes about. Whether it is heard or not does not really matter, it has the effect of stopping the person from taking any negative action because they have seen you reach for the bell or ring it. It is often just enough to prevent them either from or molesting you or, in extreme cases, from attacking.

How do we judge success?

As I began to work with clients, and to compile this handbook, I became aware of how much of the information I was receiving from all sources, internal and external, seemed ethereal and based on complex interactions. I wondered what measures of success I could apply to my work. I asked the Arimathean:

Q: How do I judge success? Is it just by the outcome? Do I just look at the client and think: 'You are getting better'?

A: Success is how people view what is taking place. You, for example, may feel you have been very successful in creating the possibility for a disease to go into remission. Someone might come with quite a virulently growing cancer, say of the breast. Their mental outlook, their fear principle might be very great indeed, and you begin on a course of crystal healing over maybe five or six weeks, fairly frequently. At the end of that time you may see a calmer person, you may see a less angry, inflamed breast. Although the cancer is still there, it has quite obviously slowed down, maybe the scans show this and the doctors are quite pleased. But your patient might be resentful and angry because the cancer is still there, because you have not reversed the situation, because it has not completely calmed and gone away. You would consider it is a good result, the doctor might feel quite amazed that there is any remission at all, and yet your patient goes away saying: 'She is not much good as a healer, I've still got the cancer, I'm still likely to die from it.'

In another scenario you might be looking for a more positive result, you might feel that the cancer is looking far too angry and there has been very little result from all your efforts, but the patient is not in pain, they feel much calmer, more peaceful and they may be very satisfied with that result, while you are resentful that you have not achieved more.

So it is an unknown variable. You cannot say because a certain group of crystals are used over a certain time, that you will get x or y as a result. This is where the personality of the individual plays such a prominent part. This is where the predominant colour in the aura, if you are able to assess it, plays an important part in divining their nature and perhaps provides you with an idea of what their mission in life actually is. Different results can depend on how their personality relates to the monthly grouping that they have been born into, whether they are Sagittarius, Cancer or Gemini. By being aware of the nature of the signs and comparing that to what you know of your patient, you can guess at what result you are likely to see after a certain period of time and whether they are likely to accept the healing or not. All of these things do have their place and should be recognised.

Q: Is healing ever impossible because the soul has chosen to learn from the illness, when death is part of the plan and not a failure?

A: That is a very interesting question, mainly because all healing is worth under-

taking. Whether someone is terminal or not, there is a great degree of peacefulness that can be attained from a healing session, maybe an upliftment which could help the sufferer to go forward towards the completion of their life without feeling so desperate or suffering so much pain. We would never withdraw healing until life itself is completely extinct.

There is not any real way of the healer knowing whether it is going to be worthwhile or not, which is a good thing, we feel, because if there were definite indications that the healing was not going to work, that could create despondency and possibly a lackadaisical attitude within the healer, let alone a feeling of 'Why bother?' in the patient. So there is no way of telling, unless the healer has asked a spiritual guide and received a rather sad reply, but we would always say that it is worth endeavouring to uplift.

Q: So even where the client might not live, is it really about creating a bridge, providing that human contact and staying the course with them, wherever that course might lead, is that it?

A: *That is so, we have often found that where there is a feeling of hopelessness, a lack of belief, a sense that when the soul reaches the end of that path there is just a blank after death, this results in fear. But a good healer, speaking a little upon the soul and the afterlife can bring about a contentment, which even at the last moment can be so very uplifting for the personality. Generally speaking, the most wonderful purpose of any healing is to enable the cessation of pain at any level.*

In discussions with Elijah we once asked him if there is any such thing as a disease or condition which was incurable?

E: *The simple answer is yes. A few diseases, the degenerative ones, simply eat away the system. There is no way, even with the most magnetic of healings, that all of a sudden everything that has deteriorated can become whole. We do not have a miracle worker within the world now that has the direct link with the God force that can do this. There are many wonderful healers who can stop the degeneration but they cannot restore those tissues, or limbs, or whatever else may have already deteriorated. Medicine can do much, medicine can replace, but at present there is no such thing as miraculous healing. But the disease, however bad it is, can be halted, with the help of the person themselves. With their real determination to carry on living, to recover, they can buy themselves extended time. They do not necessarily have to go on to the bitter end, as it were, and die because of their disease. So it isn't a categorical 'yes' or 'no'. There have been some cases where quite serious conditions have been overcome through positive thought.*

Distant healing

We prefer the holistic healing approach. You would take into yourself the Christos, mentally pass it through the crystal, into the crystal on the other side of the divide, and then visualise the Christos, magnified greatly through the energies of the two crystals, flooding through the body of the patient.

The Arimathean

Distant healing explained
As part of her research for *The Way of Diet and Health*, Rosalind Pencherek asked the Arimathean how distant healing works. Here is his explanation:

Distant healing uses a vibration which is universal and directs it into those areas or parts where it is most needed. You are 'harnessing' it, this we feel is the operative word. You harness a particular energy and direct it specifically to where it is needed to be able to function to its fullest extent. That harnessing of energy is done in cooperation with the spiritual forces and cannot be done purely and simply by the will of man.

Man can make a request, he can link himself mentally with the spirit forces and request that certain energies encircle those that are sick to give them the best possible chance to use nature's energy in order to restore themselves. Man is of nature, therefore everything that is natural supports man, enables man to overcome that which is a destroying force, that which is negative and which prevents him, either through his own mental attitude or through circumstance, from being restored to full health.

Sometimes within man it is the inability to accept or to believe that such forces can unite and be of real benefit that holds him back. If his lack of belief is very strong, it blocks the energy would otherwise penetrate, and could enable his soul structure to commune with nature's energy, to become involved with it and invigorated by it. If this happens it starts the natural process of cell multiplication and regeneration within the body.

There are two ways to do this: one is to enable mankind to appreciate that there is a life force outside of himself which can be utilised for his own regeneration and to put away from him that which is destroying, ageing or degenerative. This of course can be done through words, through counselling, but it can also be done through helping the person's soul to communicate with spirit on a spiritual level and to accept these energies which are directed towards him. This is an essential mental step within the healing process.

It can be assisted through the power of crystals or it can be reached purely through the power of the mind. But it is the connection on a spiritual level with first the inner soul aspect of the person in need and then the entire Higher Self of that personality which establishes how this power can be utilised.

When this has been done at the beginning of the healing session, then a crystal can be chosen as the medium through which the energy will pass, and connect with the awakened soul within the personality in order to receive light. Within that light is exactly the right energy level which will begin the healing process.

There are different forms of crystals that can be used for different illnesses but if you are undertaking a general absent healing, to facilitate the restoration of energy, to enable the whole body simply to regenerate, we suggest the clear quartz crystal, as clear as possible, with little movement within it.

The work of angels

When he speaks of connecting to the spirit forces, he is actually referring to the work of the angels, and therefore I include a brief extract from one of his teachings on angels. It is angels who carry the healing web of energy between the healer and the client during a distant healing.

The hierarchy of angels, as we refer to them, began as the first beings of light, many millions of years ago when the souls were first manifest as living vibrations within the universe. They were born from the silence which was created by the God force. That silence contained all knowledge, it was complete within itself, but it needed voice so that, as other beings came into life, they would be aware of this knowledge. The angels, firstly the archangels, obtained this knowledge. Originally there were twelve, but after the millions of years of existence, there are now seven, each of whom rules a different period of time within the ages as they come into being. (The recent change from the Piscean age to the Aquarian age means that Archangel Uriel – Amethyst – has now stood back and Archangel Michael – Golden – has moved forward.)

Beneath the archangels, each of whom has their specific colour and ability to rule the world during the different ages, come the messenger angels which do their bidding. These are responsible for all the healing vibrations which are within the universe and which need to be channelled in order that humankind may maintain a healthy constitution. These angels do not depend on healing vibrations from man to man, they weave the intricate patterns of light which man infuses into himself throughout his life. As he is aware of living, he is aware of light, and within that light are the healing rays which constitute his being.

The cherubs and the seraphim all have their messenger tasks. Mostly it is at the bidding of the other angelic forces, but man is able to reach these beautiful beings of light with his own thoughts, his own request that health, well being or love be sent as a thought message to others. This transference of thought is partly achieved by the cherubs, and partly through man's own life force.

So that is the hierarchy of angels. Some can be seen, indeed if this were not so, artists over the many centuries would not have been able to depict them with the brush. Those that have vision often see them as a beam of light which dances within a room, creating harmony and love within it and amongst those that dwell there.

Undertaking distant healing using crystals

What follows is the basic teaching given by the Arimathean on how to undertake distant healing using crystals:

Through the mind make the link.

Hold a clear quartz crystal, dedicated to this task, either to the brow or a little way from the forehead and concentrate on directing the energy from your third eye through the crystal.

Evoke within the mind a picture of the person who needs the healing. It is not necessary to know that person, or to have seen them, the visualisation is purely on a soul level. It is not necessary to visualise their features or the structure of their body.

Then begin the distant healing. Send several waves of energy through the crystal, and visualise it reverberating throughout the structure of the recipient.

After a few minutes give thanks to the healing forces for their intercession, for their ability to be able to connect with the tissue of the body, the tissue of the mind and the crystalline structure within the quartz crystal.

As a point of interest, Rosalind, who received this teaching, then asked if this method of healing was used during the time of Atlantis and he confirmed that it was virtually the same.

The use of crystals within distant healing

The methods of using crystals within distant healing vary according to the way in which the healing is being conducted:

If they are linking with you and you have discussed with them a procedure for absent healing, then that procedure would be different from thinking to yourself 'I will send some healing to patient no. 1, 2 or 3 to augment what takes place when they are here in the sanctuary'. If they are linking with you, then they should have a stone of similar quality to that which you would use in the sanctuary as the starting point when sending the energy.

So let us say that you are using a smoky quartz, they should hold a similarly sized and energised piece of smoky quartz themselves. Both of you should sit with a lighted candle in front of you. In actual reality, time and distance departs, and you will be sitting face to face, as the energy bridges any gulf between you when it passes from your smoky into your patient's smoky, as if there were no distance at all.

This is an exercise in mind control; forget physics and distance, forget your belief that you need to see and speak with each other in order for the energy to reach out and truly help the sick person. The distance between you is not a barrier to success, except in your minds, so both of you should visualise being in close proximity, one to another, in order to help you accept that absent healing truly works.

You can, if you wish, have one of your particularly nice crystals somewhere within the space near to you. If you want to, you can visualise the energies from that crystal coming into your specimen crystal, your smoky, and then see it pass towards the smoky that your patient has.

You can visualise a circle of light, a circle of energy which increases as the spiral begins to turn. You can incorporate anything else you wish in this. You can ask the crystal before you begin the healing to truly link, to be part of the essence of the patient, stating the illness that is prevalent. If you have chosen well and your crystal is harmonising, it may be already working on a different level within the healing, then that is all to the advantage of the patient.

It is amazing how close you can feel to someone when you are doing absent healing in this way. You can feel them, you are almost aware of their breath, you can feel their thoughts and what is even more important, you can sense if they are absent, if they have forgotten or are late, and you can perhaps sit back and wait, sending a thought in your mind, reminding them of the time that you have arranged. It is a very good exercise in concentration, or even in communication between you and your patient.

Q: When you are doing the linking, should you concentrate on linking their crystal to your crystal and allow their body to pick up the energy it needs from the crystal, or would you concentrate your thoughts on different parts of their aura? For example, prior to the healing, should I use my pendulum to pinpoint any areas of depletion or illness within the aura?

A: *We prefer the holistic healing approach. You take into yourself the Christos, mentally pass it through the crystal, into the crystal on the other side of the divide, and then visualise the Christos, magnified greatly through the energies of the two crystals, and flooding the body of the patient. You can, if you wish, see it going through at the level of their feet and spiralling upwards to a point above the head. Whichever way you do it, use a holistic approach.*

Q: So if you are not actually linking with your patient, would it be preferable to use smaller crystals or tumblestones?

A: *Yes, if it is someone whose name you have been given, that a friend or a relative is worried about, then set up your power crystal* (a working stone usually within a sanctuary, that is dedicated for general healing) *an hour or two before* *you are doing your healing. Place one or two crystals around it, having first divined which ones the pendulum feels it would be better to use for that person and particularly for the illness that they are suffering from.*

Then light your candle, sit quietly and meditate for a few minutes. Visualise what the colour of your patient is likely to be.

Wait until you see that colour come into your vision or feel it according to the way you work. Having established their colour, either by seeing or feeling the deep rose pink, or because someone has told you to use the rose pink, blue, green or whatever colour, then send that colour and the energy from your chosen crystal into the colour vibration of your unseen patient. Visualise all of the brilliant colour that you have manifested turning in a spiral from their feet up to their head and beyond. If you feel that the colour is very weak, then give it vibrancy, give it energy, because it is probably the lack of this which is causing their malady.

Q: Can you do any damage by getting the colour wrong?

A: *The only damage you could do, if damage at all, is a lack of success because it isn't really matching up very well, it's not very fluid.*

Q: So if I visualised somebody as pink and they were actually blue, it wouldn't go to the next pink person passing by?

A: *Definitely not, but have more faith in your helpers that they would transmit the right colour mentally to you.*

Q: Because I don't see anything, sometimes I find it difficult to trust.

A: *Then get them to shout in your ear 'Yellow with blue edges', or whatever it might be!*

Q: I usually get the information, it's just not confirmed by sight.

A: *Being a very factual person, this is what you are seeking, is it not? So one of your lessons is to learn to accept from spirit, and not always want a living back-up. You might be quite surprised when you meet that person ultimately, you will look at them and speak to them, and you will say, 'Oh yes, very blue'.*

Safety note:
Please do not use a crystal pendulum over a photograph of a person. Using a crystal pendulum over a photograph is an imperfect technique as you cannot guarantee pinpoint accuracy because of the size of the image. As we have already mentioned, spinning a pendulum directly over the chakras, even when in a photograph, can cause problems.

Chapter 11

Directory of crystals and their suggested uses

Because crystals are living objects they are constantly changing their internal vibrations, and as they do this they allow light, particularly sunlight, to lodge within and to move around, creating these rainbows and these beautiful shafts of light.

Elijah

Key attributes
In addition to the information on crystals for healing, the Arimathean gave the following advice on some of the key attributes of other stones, for people to purchase when they are starting to appreciate crystals and want to have some in their home. Here is the information that he provided:

Amber: Useful for removing inflammation from joints, some practitioners actually rub amber on the joints: *It would have to be the Russian amber. Many people say that it is just plastic but that is because it has got a warmer feel. It has also got a lot of movement and vibrancy. The Polish amber is more solid; it is rather more of a gold colour or yellow colour with very little in the way of flecks or anything that establishes a healing pattern. It is very good to wear, a very non-reflective stone that most people can wear without getting a negative reaction, but the Russian amber is the beautiful variety.*
Aventurine: has a calming and balancing quality which assists in meditation.
Cloudy quartz: (especially Madagascan) has a protective quality towards people. For example, I carry one in my car.
Citrine: has a vibration which is clear and energetic and can therefore assist in achieving clarity of mind and decision-making.
Fluorite: has a calming and a balancing quality, especially when it contains two colours, green and purple, then it can help to raise consciousness.
Green calcite: has calming, balancing, absorbing qualities, which can assist meditation and, by being carried in their presence, to calm people who are mentally ill.
Hematite: has a deep and a solid energy which can help to ground someone.
Jade: with its balancing and absorbing energy can assist in treating cancer.
Lapis lazuli: has a profound energy which assists in deepening the consciousness and can help in mediumship and to provide psychic protection. If a necklace of lapis, that does not include metal, is worn when using a computer, it can absorb the radiation. (Treat as obsidian, page 72, when cleansing.)
Labradorite: a steady energy which has assisted healing joints in an elderly person following an operation.
Mahogany obsidian: *This is not a pure obsidian, it is a derivative of obsidian which has a mineral which it has drawn toward it from the bed where it was pro-*

duced. We would say that it is iron that has given this type of crystal its unusual texture and shade. If you compare it with a piece of pure black obsidian, not the kind that is known as snowflake, and, with your eyes closed, feel just with your fingers, then take the mahogany in one hand and the black in the other. The mahogany has a much softer texture and with of its iron content it is a remedy for the body, not to be used to absorb radiation from equipment.

You suggest the kidneys. We would agree that certainly it can be used for that but we would also suggest the thyroid. The deficiency of iron can lead to the thyroid malfunctioning. As there is iron within this particular stone, if it is placed near the thyroid gland, to the left or the right of the neck within your layout, it should have quite a stimulating effect.

Malachite: has a energy which is absorbing, calming but also stimulating and so can help to sharpen the senses or overcome tiredness. May help to reduce stress by transmuting the heavier energies. Can assist in regression. Do not drink as an elixir as it can impart copper carbonate into the water.

Moonstone: has a gentle and often uplifting energy which helps to make a strong connection with the spirit spheres.

Moss agate: in general the darker, more vibrant green stones absorb and transmute the heavier negative energies. I tend to see the lighter green stones as assisting in meditation and the deeper green stones, such as moss agate, as absorbing stress and negativity.

Obsidian: is volcanic glass and both the rainbow and snowflake varieties can assist in improving alertness and aiding concentration. It may also be used to absorb radiation from computers and televisions (see cleansing details on page 72). Snowflake obsidian has been recommended to me in the past for psychic protection. Obsidian sheen has the quality of strength as illustrated in this advice from the Arimathean: *Obsidian has qualities of mineral rather more than crystal so it is more specifically for areas of consciousness. We suggest that it is used to stimulate brain function as well as to provide protection for those that are drawn toward it, depending very much on what variety of obsidian is being used and for which purpose.*

We find the snowflake is ideal for concentration and it also keeps evil spirits at bay. If a room has been used for a wrong purpose, it can be placed within the area of a window to prevent evil forces entering a property or to locate them in a particular area so that they do not move into other rooms or spaces within that property. The golden obsidian, with that wonderful delicate goldenness shining from it, is ideal for concentration, for allowing people to read, absorb, cut themselves off from the thoughts of others to concentrate on what they are doing. A ball of this, for they are usually shaped into ball-like shapes, is ideal for this particular work, but for other things we do not usually recommend them.

Pyrite: has an absorbing and grounding quality which can aid stress reduction.

Red jasper: is generally a grounding stone, but in its rough form it can be used as an elixir to improve kidney function.

Rutilated quartz: the combination of two crystals makes this stone very versatile. Sometimes I use it in preference to clear quartz, because it has all the qualities of the clear quartz with, in my view, added strength. The Arimathean recommends rutilated quartz for the protection of property, any inflammation of the chest or throat and to augment a Craniosacral treatment (page 86).

Serpentine: when used at the crown chakra, can impart peace and balance, as part of a healing layout. Because of its colour and its smoothness it is ideal for meditation and can be used to cleanse the blood following an infection.

Tiger's eye: there can be a mixture of energies within this type of stone which usually lends itself towards grounding, or to protect property.

Tourmaline (black) also known as schorl: a very absorbing stone which can create a feeling of drawing energy through the body. I only use it at the feet. Rosalind places it at the feet of people who are anaemic.

Quartz with moss inclusions: *This combination helps to clear the system of different poisons and toxins that collect in the intestines and the lower chakras of the body. Therefore you would probably use these crystals below the waist and can place them around a chair if the person is sitting.*

Types of Crystal

Man-made

You can purchase crystals which are man-made. The one I have is very clear, like glass. They can come in any shape or size, and can be bought from crystal dealers, who may not always know that they are not natural. Because they have so little energy I have always kept them separate from my 'natural' crystals, and the Arimathean explains why:

We are aware that there is one particular crystal that has not developed naturally from the caves either below the surface nor yet above it. The energy from this crystal is very muted, it will not last, it has been grown by man in order to produce an effect. As such crystals grow, they are moulded into whatever shape the person who is making them desires. Sometimes they are successful, other times such growths can break or be flawed.

Elijah has requested that you keep crystals such as these away from the others as they can influence their energies. There is no reason why you cannot use them at different times for a specific task, but if they are kept with genuine crystals that have a specific purpose because of their nature, it can detract from the energies that they receive during the times of the full or new moon or through the rays of the sun. Do not place the man-made ones in sunshine; you might find that they become extremely cloudy and lose what little life energy they have.

Elijah has said that this quality of absorption can be used to remove energies within the Metamorphic technique on page 131.

126

A mixture of crystal and mineral

In the extract below the piece of rose quartz that Elijah is referring to looks very similar to most medium-sized-pieces a little dense in some parts and lighter in other, but the mineral to which he refers is not visible. I include this teaching because I think it is interesting to hear how the presence of a mineral alters the function of a crystal:

This particular rose quartz has another form of crystal, with a different energy pattern within it, which has grown inside the rose quartz. This combination could create confusion if were to use this piece of rose quartz for the same illnesses or conditions as you would any other piece.

The combination of minerals alters the way that such a crystal should be used. We would suggest this one is used as a protective influence within groups where perhaps there is teaching taking place and many people are gathered. It can have a central place where that particular part of the crystal is toward the lecturer.

What has occurred here is that a smaller crystal – more of a mineral, in actual fact – was growing very near to the rose quartz. Over the many hundreds of thousands of years that the rose quartz was developing, it became centralised, or near enough centralised within it. These types of stone are quite rare and have a very strong protective energy. If you find one that has this anomaly within it, then you have done very well because they are exceptionally rare.

Laser crystal

A laser crystal could be described as a crystal wand which forms naturally. Its structure means that it is very powerful – Elijah uses the word 'activated' – and when he talks about it being carved, he does not mean by man, but by its growth formation. The end result does appear carved into a shape which resembles a finger.

This is a powerful crystal which is quite long. It can be from 6 to 8 inches (15 – 20 cm) *long and is carved in such a way that it is symmetrical all the way round, usually with six facets. Both ends of the crystal should be terminated. If it is activated and used with apparatus which enlivens the crystal, and if you were able to see what was happening inside, you would actually see energy pass along the length of the crystal, thus giving it the possibility of endless permutations of healing.*

You must be very careful with the laser. We are not terribly happy with using them too often with crystals as this breaks down the molecular structure in the other crystals and you may very well find they do not last as long as normal. No crystal lasts for years when it is used regularly; it is better that you have two or more of a similar structure so that you can rest them and then alternate them.

It is important to analyse how strong the laser is that you are preparing to use and on what person or on which stones. Some of the lasers have properties within them, that if they were used on another stone might structurally destroy it, or at least interfere with its own energies.

A laser has a specific purpose, and that is to fuse, so when you use a laser you are in effect fusing two things together. Now if you take a laser to this stone that we are holding here, there is nothing in there to fuse. There is some energy which has developed and multiplied through its use and its purpose, so what might happen is that the laser could move through the layers of crystal, which are very finely packed – there are probably something like five hundred layers of crystal in here – and it would move through it just like a beam of light into the centre – crack! So you really have to be careful how you use it, and with which crystals.

It wouldn't do that to a very big crystal, it would just make a crack in the centre of that crystal and then it could re-fuse the two together; but with a smaller crystal especially one which is very glass-like and clear, it could simply crack it, and that would spoil it.

Now when you use such a laser on humankind, keep it moving. Remember that if you are using it over areas of the body where there has been pain or illness, then all the while you are using it, you are fusing together things which have become ruptured, you are helping them to heal, but if you use it on a healthy body, you could be causing trouble.

Not all lasers do this, some of them are quite innocuous really, but then they are usually not proper lasers, they are just something that someone thinks might be a laser, and so has called it that. The real lasers are very rare indeed. When you try to pick them up and hold them you find you cannot easily do so. These are the real ones and you should be very, very careful with these, is this understood?

When Elijah came to talk to the group of crystal healing students, (the full transcript of this talk appears as Appendix 1) he emphasised his concern even more, ending with this phrase:

So we do ask that you learn how to use a laser and on which part of the body to use it, otherwise don't even contemplate purchasing one or using it.

Elestial

In some countries this is known as a 'window crystal', but this is not to be confused with the small windows which appear on quartz crystals and which are touched on briefly below. All the elestials I have worked with have been smoky, and the pattern which forms on them, and within them, I would describe as a computer circuit board; small oblong shapes which join together in an intricate pattern. Where you have a clear elestial you can see this pattern throughout the whole crystal like a 3D maze, as if the crystal is growing from the inside out, forming many small facets, which are adhering to a mineral base.

It has a very potent energy for reducing growths within the body, and I have tended to be a little cautious about using them, although I am equally fascinated by them. I have used one for fibroids, but not for any other growth as yet. When I placed it under the bed I was advised by the Arimathean to remove it immediately if the client reported any feeling of dragging. She did, quite quickly during the first couple of treatments, and then did not mention a dragging sensation again in later sessions

Q: What is the healing power of the elestial?

A: It is what is placed within it when it is used. Many have such a wonderful aura which begins to infiltrate into the appreciation of those who see its beauty. It is the energy of the healer that reaches out towards such a crystal which infuses into it the desire to share, to bring forth its healing potential, so in a way it absorbs from those that handle it, those that use it, rather than the other way round.

Q: Are you saying that it's more of a partnership, whereas the other crystals have an innate purpose that you are almost trying to divine?

A: Yes, we would agree with that.

The importance of windows and rainbows

The group of people who met with Elijah would often be asked questions about the different structures in crystals because so much is written about windows, rainbows, devic temples and 'walls' that divide some crystals, so we thought we would ask how best to advise people:

Quite honestly, if you told them the truth it would indeed burst a lot of bubbles. There really isn't any significance in any of these things within a crystal, except to add to its aesthetic beauty. People see this, they think: 'Oh, how beautiful', it is like one little piece of glass which is reflecting light all around, and very often they think there must be three or four of these, and that they must have a purpose, some real meaning, but they do not. So many of these 'windows' have been literally carved by those that prepare the crystals for sale.

A rainbow is a little different; a rainbow does grow into the crystal as time passes. Its root is there and if held in the right way into the light, almost from the beginning you see this beautiful colour resonating before your eyes. After you have used the crystal or possessed the crystal for quite a while, the rainbow will grow. Because crystals are living objects they are constantly changing their internal vibrations, and as they do this they allow light, particularly sunlight, to lodge within and to move around, creating these rainbows and beautiful shafts of light. In a dark room usually they won't show up at all; if they did, then that would be a beautiful thing to have on show, but usually they pick up their light from outside light conditions, so if you were to put them in a box and leave them there for, say, a year, the rainbow would vanish. So beyond the aesthetic beauty there isn't really any purpose in choosing crystals because of shape or light, windows, devic temples or anything else.

But we are not saying that you should not choose your crystals for their beauty, of course you should. There is so much pleasure to be had from displaying either a group, or a single crystal, especially on one of your light boxes so that all the beautiful energies inside are highlighted. It does you good, it heals you just to look at it. So we are not saying it is rubbish, we are saying don't buy your crystals for that purpose, buy them for the resonation inside your self. That means something, 'I want to use it for this, for its softness, its hardness, its energy'.

Q: There is one type of quartz crystal which has a natural diamond shaped window, usually along one edge and towards the tip of the stone. I understood that this made it easier to programme or dedicate is that so?

E: Ah yes, that is so, but you have to be very accurate in diagnosing each crystal, and what has occurred before it came to you. We are thinking rather more of your clients who come and say: 'Oh, how beautiful is this, or that' and then, not knowing anything at all about how to use them, they could use it for the wrong purpose, thinking they had a much stronger crystal than they have really got.

Using crystals within the workplace
As part of my work is within organisations, I asked about the role of crystals in the workplace and in conferences or teaching environments. The Arimathean's reply was as follows:

Have crystals within the area where you will be working. They do not have to be prominent, but they do add dimension to what will be taking place in business conferences and in areas where you will be discussing your work with interested parties. So you do not need to fear derision from those people who do not see the worthiness of crystals. You could carry one within your purse, suitably wrapped.

We suggest that a piece of gold calcite would be best for this particular function. Size does not matter, it can be extremely small. As we have said before, it is not the size of the crystal or the mineral which helps it to function. So a small piece is sufficient for you to carry with you. Another colour which helps with confidence is a very deep gentian blue as this radiates the mind function and also contains spiritual energies, so these two blended together will help with your achievement.

On another occasion he suggested that I take citrine to assist with decision-making, obsidian for its absorbing qualities and clear quartz for energy. I find if I take a small collection, people relate to different qualities within the stones and the comparison evokes lively discussions.

In one meeting I split the groups into Amethyst who took responsibility for clearing out the past; Citrine who took responsibility for ensuring the group reached decisions; Clear Quartz who made sure that the energy of the group kept flowing; and Obsidian who made sure that we stayed on task and dealt with any negativity.

Using stones with the Metamorphic foot technique

The Arimathean has mentioned combining crystals with the Metamorphic foot technique. It was a very brief reference and so I checked with him how it might work in practice. Do you, for example, use the stone on the foot or around the feet? Do you touch the feet with the crystals, or have them by the bed, or under the bed as in a Craniosacral treatment (mentioned on page 86)?

The healer can hold the crystals in the palm of their hand so that their fingers are still able, more or less, to spread out. They could take one stone in each hand and gently skim just above the surface of the skin between the knees and the feet, along the perimeter, under the toes and across the top, to allow the crystal energy to permeate into the aura of the foot, but without actually touching it. The crystals can then be laid down just outside of the toes to provide an energy support while the therapist is working directly on the feet.

In a separate teaching Elijah was asked to describe the crystals to use at the feet:

All those crystals which you would naturally use to ground humanity, to allow the awareness of an earthing process to take place, would be eminently suitable to use on the feet. Where the colour of the crystal is concerned, we would say that, for example, a jasper, which has some orange and deeper red tones mingled in with it, would be ideal to use on the feet.

In some areas of the feet you could use an obsidian, especially if you feel the person needs a lot darker energies cleared from within their aura. If they have been using energies of the occult, for example, then the obsidian is an excellent stone to use in the first one or two sessions of Metamorphic massage.

Otherwise, you can always use the familiar and beautiful quartz crystal – not the very clear quartz, use the milky quartz, one that you cannot see through, that is not transparent. The cloudy quartz crystals relate much better to that which is in close proximity to the earth.

Q: Could you use black tourmaline (schorl) around the feet?

E: Indeed you could use that.

Q: Smoky quartz?

E: How smoky?

Q: Well, not the ones that have been cooked, the ones that are natural but as dark as possible.

E: It would be those that have been 'cooked', as you put it, that would be the most suitable. The darker the better.

Q: Do man-made crystals have any part to play here?

E: Ah, yes!

Q: But they are completely clear, Elijah, they have no energy in them.

E: Sometimes you need something with no energy in it to draw out the problems.

Q: But they've almost been banned from my healing room. Are you telling me I'm going to have to allow them back in?

E: You can allow one back in, the poor little thing, allow it to be there for when you have a client that you realise has been dabbling in the wrong energies and you want to draw them out through the feet.

Q: Should you clean it in the normal way?

E: You can do that, but the cleansing of an artificial crystal is not as important as the cleansing of the natural ones.

Combining crystals with Reiki

Many of the people who I work with are Reiki practitioners and they are interested to know how they might combine their interest in crystals with Reiki. I asked the Arimathean for his advice:

Very broadly speaking, Reiki doesn't really lend itself to blending particularly well with crystal healing because the principles behind the two are very different. Broadly, crystal healers rely more on the power of the crystals and their interaction with the Earth and the client, whereas Reiki depends rather more on knowledge, and the ability of the healer to channel, through the vibrations of the body, their knowledge towards the person needing healing. We would advise Reiki healers, who want to use crystals, to hold a simple one in the palm of their right hand in order to intensify their own energy, that which they are calling upon to help their client.

Q: A clear quartz?

A: *It doesn't have to be absolutely clear, it can have a certain milkiness, but it would be wrong to use the very heavy or dense crystals, because they are either for protection, which means they would keep the energies out, or for meditation, which isn't really what you need when healing.*

One Reiki healer, who asked the Arimathean about using crystals to enhance her distant healing sessions, was advised to use three clear quartz wands. Either all the same length, or one long wand and two shorter ones. She was advised to place the wands in the shape of an arrow head, pointing away from herself, and to direct the healing energy along the wands.

The crystal systems
The shapes of crystals are classified according to their axes and the angles between them which form the faces of the crystal. The outer shape depends on the environment, the temperature, the rate of cooling, the amount of pressure and the presence of other crystals and minerals but the internal geometry of any crystals within the same system will be identical. What follows is a very brief description of the different systems:

Cubic (three axes, all equal)
Diamond, garnet, pyrite are examples of this system.

Tetragonal (three axes, two equal, one longer. All three axes are at 90 degrees)
Chalcopyrite, rutile, zircon for example.

Orthorhombic (three axes, all different lengths, all 90 degrees)
Danburite, peridot, topaz.

Monoclinic (three unequal axes, two at 90 degrees)
Jade, kunzite, malachite.

Triclinic (three unequal axes and no symmetrical angles)
Amazonite, labradorite, turquoise.

Hexagonal (four axes, three equal and at 60 degree angles, one unequal at 90 degrees)
Aquamarine, beryl, emerald

Triganol (three axes at 60 degrees and one at 90 degrees). Sometimes listed within the Hexagonal system.
Rock crystal, quartz, tourmaline.

How the structure of crystals affect their healing properties
You can get full details of all the different systems in any geological book, but what interests me is the relationship between the structure of the crystal and its healing properties. As I have developed as a crystal healer I have started to analyse the importance of the geometry within the body and how it interacts with the structures within the crystals and the healing layouts that we create.

I asked the Arimathean once and he advised me that crystals which have a cubic structure are more definite in their structure, and in their purpose, than the crystals which come from the other systems. But he advised me against pursuing this too soon. He promised more, but for volume two.

Elijah speaks to a group of crystal healing students
February 2000

We start the session with three aums and three shekinahs, see pages 13 and 15.

E: My children Shalom and welcome! We certainly enjoyed the sound of the AUM and Shekinah and it reminded me personally of the last time that I was so greeted, which was quite a little while ago. There has been much activity taking place, both universally and with humanity. It would be difficult to describe the kind of activity that all of us have been engaged in, because of the contrast between life on Earth and life in spirit, and how very differently things are felt, seen and heard. We ourselves have a perception that mankind cannot hope to have while he on the Earth and while his soul is partly within the body and partly within the Higher Self. Death releases all of this, which is why it is considered to be a rebirth, rather than that which the soul fears. Coming into life is an unknown journey, because the aspect has not lived before, but returning to spirit is one of great rejoicing, knowing that all the experiences that have taken place can be usefully engaged upon within spirit life.

Man's connection with crystals in the past
We mention this so that you will have understanding as to our different perception of the energy of crystals. Sometimes mankind comes very close to a true understanding of that energy, but usually it is on a different vibration. Everything universally is measured by vibration. The vibration man lives with is very different from the vibration of spirit and yet, as you would rightly say, spirit being within man there must be a link. A million or so years ago there was a much greater link than there is now. Man was much closer to nature and nature was part of man in a way that has now been lost. Without the true quality of nature, including the animal and mineral world, early man would not have been able to survive.

He could tell the difference between pebbles and stones around his home, within his location, and true crystals, which were emerging even then from subterranean passages and from mountainsides and caves. It was almost as though they had voices, as though they called out to humanity. Certainly where touch was concerned there was a tremendous impact. Most of you, if you pick up a crystal now, have to functionally tune in, in order to be aware of what it is relaying to you. It is not automatic, even those that work with crystals every day have to tune in and relate to the different energy patterns that are relayed to them. For those of you who are just becoming conscious of the existence of crystals and their purpose, tuning in is the most important aspect when learning how to relate to them. Any exercises that you have been given, you should work with on a daily basis.

Becoming a crystal healer
Nobody can just become a crystal healer. The aptitude might be there, in fact if it

is not, it is rather pointless persisting in trying to learn about them, because except for an interest that you might have in their beauty, you would not be able to make use of the teaching that you have been given. It is not an automatic connection that is made; what does happen is on a subliminal level. Man does recognise what is glass and what is crystal – working crystal – with the energies within. There is more than one kind of crystal. Some can be very, very beautifully carved and prepared, and used as water carriers, jugs, vases. That is not the crystal to which we refer, nor yet is the shaped and polished glass which, with its clarity and its perfection, it can give a quality of energy which is a delight, but it is not the energy of crystal. Crystals need to be worked with and one of the first lessons after becoming aware of how to tune in to them, is to know which crystals will work with you and which are just for their beauty. There is no clear-cut answer here.

Identifying a healing crystal

You might, for example, take calcite, which is one of the favourite crystals in healing. Some crystals (it does not depend upon where in the world you find it) of the calcite variety are only for their beauty, the energy patterns within, the light that is exuded, it will not heal. Even if you broke a large piece into many, many smaller pieces it would still not respond to your desire to use it within a healing pattern; and yet another piece of calcite, maybe one of those that doesn't really please the eye, but pulsates within the palm of your hands, which almost burns the tips of your fingers, that will heal.

So don't always look for beauty, look for harmony within the self, an attraction toward the essence of the crystal. If you are looking for a stone for a particular purpose, then ask those that work with crystals within your Higher Self to come forward and guide you.

Working with guides or aspects of your Higher Self

There has been a lot of discussion over many, many years, of exactly what guides are. If you use the word in its natural context, a guide is one who links with you and helps you toward the purpose that you have chosen. But many people feel that a guide is one who takes over, whose ideas, beliefs and knowledge are far greater than the self and therefore they should be listened to at all times and their advice should always be followed. What is not always readily understood is the fact that there are different guides for different purposes.

We always call them 'aspects' because they are linked with you in a very personal way, they come from your Higher Self. The knowledge of the Higher Self is such that as each of the aspects is drawn into an earthly life, it is given a purpose for that life, so that when it returns to spirit, it should be well versed in understanding the lessons and the pathway followed in that life. The personality is never forgotten, that aspect remains exactly as it was when it was within its earthly shell, but it now relates to spirit and is more than ready to help other aspects, who are living upon the Earth, to understand and make use of their purpose.

The crystal age

This is the crystal age. It is only really in the last fifteen or twenty years that that quality within crystals has, once again, been utilised for healing. Many people over a long period of time have enjoyed looking at them and have adorned their bedrooms or their sitting rooms. Over this period of time most of the crystals have been asleep and therefore they have needed to be awakened.

Energy they are, energy they relate to, therefore the energy that enables them to wake up is very specific. It is universal energy that comes in rhythms throughout the age. Roughly fifty years ago, particular energy evoked in man the desire to purchase and enjoy crystals, ones that were pleasing to the eye rather than pleasing to the heart. Then, maybe twenty years ago, another energy entered the rhythm of the universe, which began to awaken a response within those crystals that could be worked with, that could be used for a purpose. This energy divides crystals into two categories: those that will continue to provide beauty and those that can be used to help man, mainly to heal but sometimes to aid meditation, to provide protection, to help people to be strengthened or to help their purpose in life.

All these different forms of crystals vibrate to a rhythm, to a note, that is present in them and within the universal energy which is constantly changing, revolving, evolving, moving with the rhythm of life.

From now onwards all crystals which find their way into the public domain are fully awakened for their purpose. They might be having a little rest because nobody owns them yet, but that is very different from being so asleep that whatever happens around them, they do not stir.

This has of course given rise to many people feeling that crystals are nothing but something of beauty. But those who notice the changes in relatively small pieces, see the lights, colours, the movement of energies and pictures within a crystal and could never doubt that they are alive.

How the spirit world relates through crystals

Those of us in spirit, when we come into close proximity with a piece of crystal, can actually see a living response within them. We respond to what this crystal that our medium is holding is asking of us. You might ask: 'How on earth do you do that? You might be animating her in speech and action, but how can you actually feel what she is holding?' At one time we could not, it was as though we were acting in a different sphere but relating to her sphere and enabling her to work with us, to express what we wish to say. But gradually, over a long period of time, we have become more aware of her humanity and are able to relate to it. This makes a great deal of difference, both in the way that we relate to other people who are alive and in their human bodies, as well as the way that we relate to our medium. It is as though we encompass her, and different energies and movements within her relate to our soul bodies and bring forth a response.

As she holds a crystal, she may not be aware that that crystal is talking, but we are, because the ethereal realm of the crystal energy vibrates through her, to us or to whoever is channelling through her, and that person, that spirit, is then able to do what the crystal requests. In her case she holds a self-healing crystal, so the crystal knows if she has a pain in her toe, a sore throat, or whatever it may be. The energies vibrate in a particular way which says to us: 'She needs a little more help there'. We can then channel the energy that relates to the crystal from the sphere in spirit where that energy is drawn from; this enables the crystal to work with whatever need is within her.

So if you apply the same principle to whoever is holding a crystal, whether for self-healing or to give healing to another, that crystal knows its purpose and it works through the human being, into the soul and the same action takes place. You are not overshadowed or encompassed by that energy in the same way, but the energy still vibrates to and from that sphere of light into the earth.

It is not easy to take on board straight away, you will have to think about it, but it is one of those essential elements when learning about crystals which enables you to have a greater insight into why the crystals you work with become so close, so loved, and mean so much to you. It is because you begin to mean so much to them.

Relating to the movement within crystals

Now that you know there is movement within the crystals you can, if you wish, try to be consciously aware of it. Look hard into the crystal, look at all the little energy patterns, the rainbows, the lights within it and concentrate hard to see whether you can see a flickering of energy between one little mirror and another. Then close your eyes, hold the crystal between your thumb and first finger, and concentrate on both those digits, sense what is happening to the pads of your fingers as they respond to the crystal. Sometimes people say: 'I can't work with that crystal, I love it, it seemed just right for the purpose for which I bought it, but every time I hold it I want to drop it.' Well, the crystal is telling them something. They, or the shopkeeper, might well have thought it was good for that purpose, but the crystal is saying to you: 'Use me for something else', this is why you have pendulums. The pendulum has a very particular ability to tune in. It tunes into what you are asking of it, what you want to know, and it tunes into the crystal who (we say 'who' because they are so alive) immediately reverberates back to the pendulum with its reply.

There will always be those people who will say you are mad. Maybe you are a little; that makes it even nicer when you think that you are mad in such a perfect way, relating to nature. Nobody says you are mad if you talk to your cat, your dog, or your fish, why should they? Because they actually see them respond, but does that make a difference? Your crystals may not get up and beg, but there is something within them that is responding to you, and if you feel it and you know it, then it is a wonderful sense of madness, but other people might not respond to them in the same way. So the lesson here is that if you choose certain crystals (or they choose you) to work in a certain way, don't lend them to other people. Tell them to go out, seek their own crystals, purchase them and work only with their selected stones. The lesson we are trying to get over is how personal these stones are to each individual.

You will not have received exactly the same response while you were being taught, because these crystals are more universal, they are here for that purpose. They have been cleansed, they have been energised and they are ready for you to begin to learn how to use them, but once you have your own, then your true work begins and it is better to have one crystal that you really relate to, than to have a dozen that are left upon the shelf to get dusty, that are kept in a dark place, that are never spoken to, never caressed, and what is the ultimate insult – never cleansed and never energised. Can anyone here tell me how to energise a crystal?

Answer: In the new moon and the full moon.

E: Which?

A: The new moon for the clear crystals, the ones which reflect the colour gold, and the full moon for the opaque crystals.

E: How would you know that a clear crystal reflected gold or any other colour?

A: I don't know.

E: That's honest, at least! Does anybody know? No replies.

E: We are not surprised, you cannot possibly know. The crystals within themselves know what colour they reflect, which sometimes is the same as their outer colour, but in the case of the very clear crystals, there is no outward sign of what colour they are vibrating to or why. Sometimes you have a very clear indication. You think to yourself: 'There is something within this crystal that leads me towards a particular way of healing', and then through quite a long, tortuous route, you begin to learn about beams of light, spheres of light, how different crystals react to people who come from different realms of light, but all of this is later on in your education. It is important not to try and fill your minds with too much advanced technical detail until you have completely understood the basics, the simple side of crystals and their work.

Would anybody here like to tell me what has stood out most in your mind throughout this course that you have been on. Let us go round the group and each one say what has stood out most clearly in what you have been taught.

A1: I didn't know very much about crystals before the course and so I found it interesting to learn about the power that they have. For me it is the whole appreciation of what they can do, and how they are connected with humans.

A2: For me it has been really worthwhile meeting our teacher, because she has made it easy to understand what she has taught us.

A3: I knew that I liked crystals before the course but I now feel as if I am becoming more connected to them, but at the same time I realise how much I still have to learn. Coming here, I feel very energised, after being here for the day, and now that I know more about crystals, I feel that they are helping me in some way, so I want to extend that and do it safely, and with knowledge.

E: It is interesting what you have just said about feeling the energy of them when you began the course. In a way we have been waiting for someone to say that they feel differently when they have crystals around them, compared to the times when they are not with crystals.

A4: Simplicity really. The grid and the structure that has been built upon that. It is simple and complicated at the same time and it gives a framework that sticks in your mind.

A5: Yes, I had the same thought – the simplicity of it. There is no need to have every type of crystal, and the concept of not using the crystals directly on the body, that really was very important for me to understand.

E: Very important to us also.

A6: It's been an eye-opener, I've learned an awful lot about crystals working with our teacher, because she has such an easy way of explaining things.

E: That easy way comes with knowledge, of course. It is worth noting that if any of you have in mind either to teach regarding crystals or to set up a centre or a healing clinic, either on your own or as part of a group, you should not even contemplate it until you know not just the basics, but the pitfalls.

Laser crystals

There is one pitfall that we feel we must talk about. We have known of people who have had terrible results from the misuse of crystals, even a crystal which appears inanimate within the hand, which the healer may not have energised, let alone cleansed, which in itself does create problems.

*The crystals we are thinking of are called 'lasers'. The inner power of a laser is very subtle when it is felt by the user, but can be quite deadly if it is used incorrectly during a healing. There are areas of the body that a laser should **never, under any circumstances, be used upon to give healing**, one of these is the eye.*

Lasers, whether programmed to do so or not, relate to the optic nerve. Within lasers there is a particular energy, which vibrates to light and can change light particles. When light particles fall into different groups they become objects which can be actually seen – it is the merging together of all these groupings that you and we call 'seeing'. The ability to distinguish between a crystal, a piece of glass, or any-

140

thing else, comes about because of the groupings of different energy particles according to their molecular structure.

But because of the manner in which laser crystals develop, the fact that they are naturally compacted, formed and shaped, there is an ability inherent within them to create or to destroy. If it is used for an eye condition it can destroy sight. It does not always do this; sometimes it can give a little more energy and power to the optic nerve to clear the sight and clear any problems that are preventing the person from seeing. But if it is used for too long, for more than a few seconds, it goes too far, penetrates too deeply and can change the pattern of the optic nerve which cannot then see clearly what is before it. A few more seconds, or another application, can cause scarring or burning within the optic nerve and destroy it. Once a nerve is destroyed there is nothing, as yet, that can repair it. They, crystals, are working on that, and when eventually nerves can be repaired, it will be through crystal healing that this will happen.

So we do ask that you learn how to use a laser and on which part of the body to use it, otherwise don't even contemplate purchasing one or using it.

Note from the compiler: Please use caution when using any crystals directly over the eyes. In one case crystals which were used above the eyes dried up the secretions, and caused long-term impairment. I would advise you to place your crystals in a grid around the head as shown on page 110.

E: Now, for the rest of our time with you, we will answer your questions.

Colours
Q1: I have a question about colours. In art, black contains all colours and white is basically lack of pigment, but in the spiritual tradition white contains all the colours. Could you clarify that for me?

E: This is so because in the knowledge of good and evil, white and black, you have got the opposites which reflect one way spiritually, and another way materially. So materially, when you are arranging the colours, the paint upon the easel, you are using that which is available within your secular world and therefore you are using the opposite to what would be created for you in the spirit world.

Everything that is of spirit, everything that reflects the colours that make the spectrum within light, is the reflection of what takes place upon the Earth. It doesn't matter which way you look at it, whether from a spiritual viewpoint or from a human viewpoint, it reflects in the opposite way.

Perhaps it is simpler to use the analogy of the mirror. A mirrored image is not the same as if you were able to turn round and look at yourself. You are not even looking at yourself the way others would see you. It is man-made and designed to reflect in a particular way. It is the same with a reflection of the light which comes from the spheres of light.

Travelling to your clients

Q2: I was wondering if a crystal healer who travels around to her patients would be able to create the type of healing energy that our teacher has in her healing room, with all the beautiful crystals?

E: Sometimes more successfully. When you have a great number of crystals in an area, some of which are your working crystals that you use for healing or to teach other healers, you truly need to place the other crystals that are not being used in the room into abeyance, so that they do not reflect what is taking place, or are so alert, so energetic, that they might interfere with a particular pattern of energy that you are creating.

So it can be quite difficult in a room of this nature with many different kinds of crystal. Some people would cover them over so that they were not either receiving or reflecting, while others can do this with the mind. It is very easy to use the power of the mind in order to energise crystals and to help them with their own innate power to heal.

So those who go to visit a patient and who take a selection with them, nicely arranged in a little carrying case, energised, prepared and covered individually, so that their energies do not mix and inter-relate, can have as much, or maybe more, success in using them than when there are so many which are not actually engaged in the healing act.

At this point we will ask your teacher what she does to ensure that the energies of the many crystals that she has within her healing room do not interfere with those she uses for healing?

Working in a room which contains many different crystals

A: I use relatively few healing crystals, and during a healing any that I have not selected for that particular client are put away in a cabinet with the drawers shut. Most of the crystals out on the shelves are ones that, apart from those being used during this course, have never been used in the past, so in my mind they are closed off. All of the calcites are in jars with lids on, for example, and any which are used for healing are stored separately. So the ones that have the most potential are shut away.

E: Have you included the importance of this in your course?

A: I have not, in terms of the course, or the book, because I concentrate so much on having very few crystals around, so I have really concentrated on the fact that you don't need many, rather than what to do if you have a lot.

E: If you have space, just for the sake of those who might have a lot of personal crystals and who might think that they would help with the energy, they would then realise that there can be dangers in leaving them exposed.

We know ourselves of a case where all the energy in many crystals which were in a room was completely negated because of the energy that was needed to restore health in somebody who was receiving healing. Fortunately, the healer concerned knew how to re-energise the crystals and realised something was wrong with them. But it is not everybody who would have that perception, and then they might wonder why their poor crystals had ceased to radiate their beauty.

If you tell people to cover them with silk, that would be ideal. Not everyone has the mind power to still them directly, because you have, as we explained earlier, to perceive the note that those crystals reflect upon within your own mind. It can be any colour of silk, it is just a barrier, but silk is a soft, gentle barrier.

If you want to prevent a larger crystal from drawing in energy from another source, you can use velvet, and of course the darker the colour, the greater the intensity of covering and shielding that takes place.

Boosting the immune system through self-healing

Q3: Our style of living generally leads to a decrease in our immune system, and this can lead to different illnesses and cancers. Is it the daily self-healing (page 51) that strengthens the immune system and prevents this breakdown, or is there a particular stone or way of healing that you would advise?

E: Self-healing on a daily basis is indeed crucial, so of course we would advise somebody to choose their personal crystal very carefully, go through the routine of energising it and using it regularly, with the idea of healing in mind. It is important that the person understands the relationship between crystal energy and the cellular structure, so a little teaching on that point would be required. Visualisation is important, to actually visualise the body responding to the energy of the crystal using whatever pattern, images, colours, words, the person finds the best in order to re-inforce the self-healing that is taking place.

Crystal elixirs

Other things are important – homeopathic treatment, herbal treatments, or drops obtained from using crystals which have been soaked in water for a while and their energies absorbed into that water. What some people don't realise is that it should be stored in a sealed receptacle so that the energies do not escape, don't leak out. When the crystals are removed, the energised water should immediately be put into the container that will be used and the crystals laid aside for a period of time to regain their energies and to instill once more into themselves that which has been drawn out. If this is done on a regular basis there should be different sets of crystals which can be used to keep the supply maintained. This can be an excellent way to help to limit the degeneration of certain organs.

The amethyst relates to the kidneys and calcite relates to the liver. A clear crystal is excellent with the gall bladder and continues to work even when that organ, or part of it, has been removed. This is another subject, but very briefly, after a period of time the etheric of that organ reconstitutes the entire mutilated, or operated-on, organ in order to restore the overall energy. So people who have one kidney eventually vibrate with two, and those that have had a gall bladder removed will still function in a normal way, as if it were still in situ within the body.

These other measures which help to maintain health and immunity from illnesses, have their place just as much as the self-healing. They actually help the immunity to become more robust.

Using crystals to meditate and for self-healing

Q4: When I meditate, I hold two crystals in my hands, one that is for self-healing and the other for meditation and healing for others. I'm just not sure which hand to use for which crystal.

E: If you are asking us the best way to use them, it would be separately. Ideally your self-healing, and healing for others, should not be combined. So we would say, use your self-healing crystal in the left hand, and you would find after a period of time, when you are going through your routine, that you need to put it into the right, this more or less signifies on a mental level that you have completed your self-healing. Then, if you want to do it in the same session, start off your absent healing in the left, and again go by your desire to shift it, to know that the absent healing is completed. The meditation crystal would be a third one which you could then have in front of you on your table, and in order to begin your meditation and/or complete it, you don't have to pick it up, you can just relate to it, but if you want to pick it up and hold it like this (pointing towards the chakra in the left palm).

Changes since the Millennium

Q5: I wondered if you would comment on the changes since the Millennium, two months ago. When we worked with the crystals after the new year, it felt to me that there were changes both in the human body and in the crystals. Do we need to fundamentally revise our practice?

E: You don't really need to worry. Like a lot of the adjustments that someone like myself has been involved in, we have been working very hard to unite all the vibrations on all the different levels, so that as they are raised they are coordinated. So your crystals and yourself will have moved in a pattern together, you don't have to think about raising them with thought or any kind of action – that is if we have done our work correctly, because we have been very busy for quite a while – but just be assured that whatever is evoked, or needed, by man on the Earth from the spiritual realms does have a complementary vibration. That which diminished has diminished in harmony, and that which increased has increased in harmony. Does that put your mind at rest?

Q: Yes it does. Are you in effect saying that the earlier concern that we might need to use less energy is not now so prevalent and so we can keep working in the same pattern as before the changes?

E: Virtually, yes, but we did notice that we still had work to do and will continue to work on the changes until at least the Spring Equinox. I had to have dispensation to come here today. I hope you are all duly grateful! I was delighted to be able to re-introduce myself and have a little human life around me.

Using a pendulum?
Q6: Do we need to use a pendulum, is it important?

E: If you want accuracy, yes, but don't use it for everything. Don't ask a pendulum if you should go shopping, or whether you should go by train or bus, that is not the reason for it. Crystal pendulums are tuned to a vibration that works with crystals, so if you are using a pendulum in that way, you are using it correctly. Until you are absolutely sure that your mind is adequately tuned into the crystals you are using, that you can pick up their response and know for sure what it is they are telling you, you will need to verify it with a well-cleansed and good pendulum.

Well, our signal happened (the click of the tape recorder at the end of the 60-minute tape) *so we will say farewell to you. When I use the word 'we', it is all the others that have come in to have a listen as well and to meet you, to see what it is you are so interested in and what you are learning. There are students in the spirit world as well that need to be taught and so we usually bring quite a number with us when we come to teach. They help to raise the vibrations and to enable what is taking place on a learning level to be more concentrated, and for those humans who are listening to have a better concentration within their minds. So until we meet again, our love, all of us, toward you, and may you learn, be happy in your learning and happy in your use. Shalom.*

The Children of Light

The Children of Light are already among us. They are highly intuitive, with eyes that betray an understanding far beyond their years. Their deep inner knowing and innate sense of purpose means that they don't take kindly to either direction or discipline. On the other hand they grow and glow in the presence of love.

These children, the eldest now in their late teens, are different from the rest of humanity in two important respects. Firstly, they are souls who have finished their round of incarnation and so have no karma. Secondly, they have access to the knowledge of their entire Higher Selves. They are spiritual elders, incarnating now in response to the environmental, political and economic crises that face humanity.

Why now?

During the Piscean age the development and understanding of science was brought to a pinnacle and has provided humanity with power and wealth. But the scientific approach, without being balanced by a deeper understanding of the spiritual, has brought with it the seeds of its own destruction. The first task of the Children of Light will be to address this imbalance, to restore to humanity an understanding of the laws of balance and harmony.

The Children of Light have a very specific role in relation to crystals and an ancient affinity with them and so it may well be that as you have read the book you have felt a deep resonance within yourself, or keep thinking of a child or young person who delights in crystals and seems to have an innate understanding of them.

What follows is a slightly edited version of the first trance given by Father Abraham on the subject of the Children of Light in the summer of 1998. The full series of five trances is available as one of the Arimathean Foundation monograph series, published by the Leaders Partnership (see page 159).

The origins of the Children of Light

Abraham: *It is indeed a time of great excitement that is beginning to dawn. The Children of Light, many of them are already in existence, within their souls looking forward to their tasks. Many of them are still in infancy and a little afraid of what lies before them, needing so much the hand of love from parents, teachers, guardians and friends.*

... It all began at the time of Atlantis, the great length of time that the Atlanteans slaved and worked and endeavoured to change humanity into soul-searching, light-engendering people. Not all the Atlanteans by any means lifted their faces toward the light; indeed there were many that found their purpose very difficult to engender. However, there were those that worked with crystal energy and worked also with the light streams as they encircled them, that were aware of

powerful energies within the oceans which also helped the crystals to re-energise and to form their tasks and be part of the general understanding of that time.

The crisis of Atlantis

Wonderful things were created of crystal, the caves were full of them, even the seabed was composed of many of these beautiful minerals and crystals. Then there was a choice that needed to be made. The wise ones who would visit Atlantis from their own sphere of light realised a time was coming when good and evil would fight for survival. They would come and speak to many groups in the same way as we ourselves are coming so to do. They would speak to the elders within the Temple, those that led the people and taught them as well as to those that had charge of some of the particularly potent crystals which were used for rituals and rites to lift the whole atmosphere into one of purpose and beauty.

There were those that used the rituals for darker energies and this had to be overcome. There needed to be great energies, and these energies were mostly from the oceans themselves. There was a cave; now this cave was only visible two or three times a year, when the spring tides would be prevalent. At that time chosen groups of elders would walk into the cave, and a special ritual would take place in its depths. At that time noises akin to thunder would be heard coming from the depths. They did not understand what was taking place. The elders in the spheres of light did not consider it was auspicious to tell them, in case it brought forth fear.

Then came the time when it was realised that the time of Atlantis was drawing to its close. Somehow the work had to continue, the children growing had to understand how important they were to the continuance of the tribes that lived at that time. The elders explained to them that when the time came, there would be many boats. They were to proceed to the shore, to go into those boats and in each one would be a leader that would take them away from the disaster area, to another land where they might begin again to create light and peace.

All these children had charge of particular groups of crystals; each one would adhere to a particular colour, whether blue or green or gold or deep pink, it mattered not, they accepted their task. They kept an assortment of these crystals at all times, and they became extremely aware of what was taking place in some of the groups to destroy their wonderful island. Over hundreds of years many have sought that land which disappeared under the oceans.

A great Teacher

On one of these occasions the elders from the spheres of light came in person. All these young people were bid to sit in an auditorium, to have with them one particular crystal which they could call their own. At a certain point within the ceremony they were led to the entrance to the cave. For some time this strange rumbling noise had been taking place deep within the bowels of the Earth. But they were full of enthusiasm, fear did not enter into it, they were too full of excitement and they followed their leader into the cave. This cave was on many levels, lit with flares which showed them the way down, and as they went down and round, like a spiral staircase, deeper and deeper into the Earth the rumble became louder. They walked for a long while until they were bidden to take the flares from the walls to light the path that they now descended into. The darkness was intense. There were twelve of these children. There was utter and complete silence, then they became aware of an essence of energy entering into them that they had never been aware of before. Tremendous power surged through them, an awareness of everything that had happened to them in their present life and how every aspect of soul within their Higher Selves was giving forth the memory of how and when they had lived.

It was truly beautiful and awe-inspiring, as each young person melted into the darkness and re-emerged as who they had been in a past life. They looked at each other with recognition and love by the light of their torches, so their crystals grew and magnified into pure light in their grasp. How long they were there, how long they entered into the sound of the universe – for their souls were indeed in the centre of the Earth – they knew not. They knew their purpose, they knew that who they now were would gradually change into who they would be when they were called by the Masters to serve again. It was as though they slept and when they awoke they were again in the auditorium on the island. The knowledge that had been imbued within them had made them centuries old, so wise, so sure of their purpose; they were beautiful to behold.

The downfall of Atlantis

It was not long before the event that caused the downfall of Atlantis occurred, and each as they were bidden went into their craft and were rowed away. The ancient Egyptians welcomed these children into their midst. Still those of the higher spheres would come and speak with them and be their rulers, and as each generation gave way to another the work continued. It changed greatly, it had to change with the time that needed a change, and many of them did not pass to spirit but regenerated their energies and their beings to continue with the enlightenment for all.

Then it was the time for them to return to the spirit spheres, still aware that they would be called, that their great Teacher of that time, Ahalem, who was eventually to be born as Abraham, would call them to their task. It seems almost impossible to imagine that such young children in the present day can have such a wealth of knowledge within their inner selves, but they have. They will not be bidden from their purpose, even those that are born to the uninitiated, to those that have never heard of them; as soon as they are mature enough they will find their way forward, to take others by the hand.

But this present time as they grow is so important. Waste not any opportunity to help them, let them speak with you, let them share what is in their souls. It is only by this action that many will truly understand that the world lies within their grasp. To God the Father, the world is His eldest son and therefore must be preserved for all time.

The Higher Self, soul and reincarnation
Extract from 'The Way of Love' and 'The Children of Light'.

Initially soul was one vast energy field. At a particular point in evolution this exploded into a myriad of particles which gathered together into Higher Selves. The Arimathean has often said that it is difficult to explain the true nature of the Higher Self. Language itself is based on what individuals see around them, and it is difficult to understand what cannot be perceived.

Each individual soul is an aspect or particle of a Higher Self and each Higher Self contains more particles than there are cells in a human body. Not all aspects incarnate, just as a woman has the potential to conceive hundreds of children in a lifetime and may only actually give birth to two or three children. At the end of life the individualised soul returns to the Higher Self and the experience and learning of that life is shared throughout the entire Higher Self. Once an aspect has incarnated it cannot return; each aspect or cell of the Higher Self can only incarnate once. Because of this, when a soul returns, something akin to a conference takes place where the karma is reviewed, the experiences and understanding of life are evaluated and a new aspect steps forward, with the essence of the previous life within, to take the learning forward.

If the Higher Self could be seen, it would resemble a vast rainbow, and the particles that comprise it are organised according to the colours of that rainbow, called light streams – pink, amethyst, gold, silver, green and blue and all the hundreds of shades in between. Each light stream has a different learning pattern and this pattern takes an average of two to three hundred incarnations to fulfil. Also the Higher Self can incarnate more than one individualised soul at a time. Often in the later stages of spiritual development these souls that share a Higher Self are members of the same family.

Apparently if one could see the Higher Self one would be delighted by its great beauty. The Arimathean has said:

Imagine looking at a sunset, how the sky above radiates the light, how each cloud represents a facet of the pinks and oranges, the blues and greens of the sunset; and then imagine the Higher Self.

Some may say 'but if the soul has such proportions, how is there room for so many in spirit?' But spirit is not measured by an area of space; spirit is a dimension. It is not like your world where you must travel from one place to another in order to experience the change of view, the different countries and the people dwelling in them. Spirit being a dimension of light contains all things in a comparatively small area in comparison to your world. Unfortunately to be able to visualise that which you have never seen is virtually impossible.

So a true insight into the Higher Self – the total soul – can never be achieved because it is of a vastly different vibration from that of which the body is aware.

The soul has the opportunity to learn in spirit as well as upon the Earth, but the Earth is an important school for the soul, where the Higher Self can enrich its understanding with first-hand knowledge of the full range of human emotions. Ultimately it is where the Higher Self can come to know love. It is the planet where the soul can express itself, can move forward and has that greatest blessing of all – free will. The soul in its own environment does not have free will. It has total knowledge and understanding of life and universal law; it has accepted what it is simply to be, but that is not sufficient for truly understanding the lessons that life can offer, lessons such as compassion, tolerance, understanding and patience.

When the soul enters the physical self at the time of birth, conscious knowledge of the past is concealed. Later, at different times of life, an aspect of the Higher Self that has lived before and that has an interest or karmic investment in the particular events or lessons that are being lived through will step forward to offer help, assistance and understanding. This help is often initially recognised through synchronicity, experiences of *déjà vu* or dreaming. Through meditation and spiritual development such a link with a 'spirit guide' can be built upon and even parts of the past life can be recalled. The spiritually enhanced understanding of the guide can then help the individual to go forward, develop and succeed.

For more information about crystal healing workshops contact:
The Leaders Partnership, PO Box 16457, London, SE14 5WH, UK
Web site: www.sacredstones.co.uk

Index

C

Calcification, 89

Calcite, 91, 143; blue, 91, 111; gold, 91, 111; green, 100, 102, 124; honey, 91, 93; red, 91

Cancer, 30, 47, 56, 98, 109, 111, 112, 117, 124

Candle flame, 13

Catherine wheel, 19

Cause and effect, 14

Celestite, 47, 56, 95, 111

Cell, single, 16, 17, 47, 100

Chakras, 13, 39, 41, 47, 79, 84, 95; and storing crystals, 77; balancing, using crystals, 44; base, 42; colours of, 38, 41; crown, 39, 55, 102, 109, 126; closing of, 19, 38, 105; definition of, 13; effect of crystals on, 44; experiencing the energy flow, 45; heart, 38, 40, 52, 91, 101, 115; higher, 13; lower, 13; out of balance, 59; palm, 42, 43; relationship with the meridians, 37, 46; solar plexus, 41, 79, 102; soles of the feet, 43,47; sacral, 42; third eye, 34, 35, 38, 40, 45, 61, 75, 96, 98, 101, 115, 121; throat, 38, 40; working on the 'main' five, 46

Chemotherapy, 78, 85

Cherubs, 120

Children, healing of, 80, 102, 104; of Light, 13, 22, 26, 39, 104, 114; ages of, 146; definition of, 146; Followers, 26; Leaders, 26; origins of, 146

Chinese medicine, 46

Christ, 9, 14; energy, 14, 19; light, 19

Christos, 15, 19, 38, 41, 50, 69, 99, 132; energy, 39, 80; relation to God, 14

Citrine, 89, 112; green, 90

Cloth, gold, 75; purple, 75

Colour, 10, 20, 28, 29, 31, 33, 34, 36, 38, 44, 47, 59, 64, 68, 79, 95, 113, 123, 130, 139, 141, 147; inability to visualise true, 28; kaleidoscope of, 19

Compiler, information about, 10

Computers, 72, 124, 125

Cosmic, energy, 17; mind, 20

Cosmos, 16, 20

Counselling, 118

Craniosacral, therapist, 89; treatment, 126

Creative force, 41

Creative principle, 14

Creator, 14, 29

'Crust', 72

Crystal(s), ability to rejuvenate the body, 22; agate, 125; amber, 124; ametrine, 89; amazonite, 133; amethyst, 22, 63, 69, 81, 89, 143; amplify, 70, 31, 32, 73; and aura and meridians, 36; and distant healing, 121; and light streams, 32; and man's connection with the past, 135; aquamarine, 73, 133, 109; at centre of the earth, 20; auric colour, 31, 36; aventurine, 110, 124; balancing the chakras, 44; basic healing kit, 86; beryl, 133; blue, 57, 130; Brazilian quartz, 52, 76, 87; breaking of, 20, 63, 70, 71, 73, 75; calcite(s), 57, 61, 72, 91, 124, 130, 136, 143; caring for, 70; carnelian, 79; celestite, 47, 56, 111; chalcopyrite, 133; choice of, 53, 58, 59; citrine, 79, 89, 124, 130; green, 90; cleansing, 72, 73; creating a link with spirit, 50; cubic, 133; danburite, 133; diamond, 133; directory of, 124; double terminated, 51; effects on the chakras, 44; elestial, 69, 128; Elijah, 9, 10, 12, 25, 34, 118; elixir(s), 68, 89, 125, 143; emerald, 64, 133; energising of, 73; enhancing their impact, 75; enhydro, 100; equipment, 73; established, 55; establishing a strong link, 50; fluorite, 124; for a single purpose, 59, 66; for specific illnesses, 66, 126; fountain, 76; garnet, 133; grid(s), 35, 78, 112; for basic healing, 61, 79, 91, 93, 96, 98; diagram of, 101; for eye conditions, 109; for a seated client 102, 103; for specific conditions, 111; for kidney problems, 110; protective, 84, 87, 100; healing, 53, 136; healing-diploma course, 11, 56; healer, 135; healing of children over two years old, 81; healing, what it is, 16; heart structure, 71; hematite, 124; hexagonal, 133; Higher Self of, 56; how to know if it is cleaned, 73;

W
Wand(s), 23, 36, 47, 84, **91**, 92, 100, 104, 109, 110, 112, 127, 133
Way of Diet and Health, 11, 119
Way of Love, 149, 159
Way of Soul, 14, 32, 159
Window sills, 69, 72, 73, 76, 80; crystals, 129
Women, pregnant, **79**, 80, 81, 85
X
X factor, 49
X-ray vision, 71
Y
Yeshua, 9, 14
Z
Zircon, 133

Publications from the Arimathean Foundation

The Arimathean Foundation has been established to promote and distribute the spiritual teachings of Joseph of Arimathea, Father Abraham and the Prophet Elijah, who currently speak through a deep-trance channel.

Our first publication, *The Way of Love*, is a biography of Joseph of Arimathea told through a mosaic of discussions he had with individuals about past lives that lived during the time of Christ. Through these verbatim accounts he reveals the story of his family, the events surrounding his life and those of his nephew Yeshua, who was to become the Christ.

The second book, *The Memories of Josephes*, is an intimate account of the life of the elder son of the Arimathean and his relationship with Yeshua. As children they were cousins and playmates; as adults Josephes and Yeshua were companions and confidants. The brilliant images and descriptions that make up this book are memories of a past life, recalled during meditation by the author.

The *Way of Truth* is an exposé of the enduring truth that lies behind some of the most perplexing scientific and spiritual riddles facing humanity today.

In addition to these major works, two smaller imprints have been established, the Monographs and the Healing Handbook series. The Healing Handbooks are designed to give those involved in healing and caring simple, practical insights, direct from spirit, to help them and their patients and loved ones achieve optimum health. *The Way of Crystals* is the first title in this series and gives unique and authoritative advice into the use of crystals for healing.

The Monograph series was established so that talks on specific and topical subjects from the three spiritual teachers, as well as inspired writings from the Arimathean group, could be placed before the public.

The first in the Monograph series was *The Children of Light*. This publication comprises the contents of five, hour-long discussions with Father Abraham, the spiritual leader of these children. He has set out the needs, purpose and vision of a generation of very old souls who, with our help, will restore balance, harmony and spiritual understanding to the world.

In the second of the Monographs, *The Way of Soul*, this time based on six talks, Joseph of Arimathea presents a major thesis on soul: what it is, where it comes from, its relationship to God and to humanity, the vital importance of soul in this age and most importantly the pathway of soul, known since the beginning of time as 'The Way'.

In *Discourses with Malachi* a new spiritual teacher is introduced to our publications. Over the course of four years Malachi spoke to David Davidson during meditation and this extraordinary dialogue, which gives explanations about spiritual development and insights into the process of inspired channelling, is gathered in this book.

For a full list of publications available from the Arimathean Foundation write to: The Leaders Partnership, PO Box 16457, London, SE14 5WH, UK.